SSAS PENSIONS

**CREATING EXTRAORDINARY LEVELS
OF COMPOUNDING WEALTH**

CONTENTS

Research by Mark Stokes & Nigel Greene

Cover Design by Avnie Shah

Email: mark.stokes@equaSSAS.co.uk

www.SSASalliance.org

www.markstokesuk.com

Printed and Bound in the UK by Book Printing UK

SSAS

ALLIANCE

DISCLAIMER

The information in this book does not constitute financial or other professional advice and is general in nature. It does not take into account your specific circumstances and should not be acted on without professional advice from a fully qualified and independent financial adviser who should have a full understanding of your current situation, future goals and objectives.

Although the author has made every effort to ensure that the information in this book was correct at the time of printing, the author does not assume, and hereby disclaims any liability to any party for any loss, damage or disruption caused by errors or omissions, whether such errors or omissions result from negligence, accident or any other cause.

The author is not an Independent Financial Advisor nor is he regulated in any way by the Financial Conduct Authority, and no inference should be taken in this book to suggest to the contrary.

DEDICATION

I would like to dedicate this book to my wife, Sharon, for her wonderful support, love, companionship and energy as well as to my four children: Ben, Jack, Katy and Emily who make me so proud.

They are my constant in life, my reason 'why' and who I firmly believe have the potential to make a positive change in the world and achieve great things.

ACKNOWLEDGEMENTS

There are many people who have had a profound effect and impact on my life; some remain great friends, others I have met briefly on my journey of life and others, sadly, are no longer with us today.

I would like to thank my family for their strong support, guidance and love and who have spurred me on to write this book and achieve the best I can in life. Sharon, Ben, Jack, Katy and Emily I love you more than words can say.

To my business partner in our EquaSSAS business, Nigel Greene - your ever-present companionship, friendship, drive, counsel and wisdom has been a constant source of inspiration to me.

To Avnie Shah - for your wonderful support, counsel and amazing work once again in designing another great book cover. Your patience and insightful questions continue to be a revelation to me and have been immense in creating truly professional artwork.

A big thank you to Naz Stewart and the team at Book Printing UK whose patience, expertise and wisdom has been invaluable yet again, in bringing this book to fruition.

And finally, and with a heavy heart, my great friend Pete Abbott who is sadly no longer with us, passing away only weeks before his SSAS was to be approved. Pete had so many rare qualities and was an incredible guy, a wonderful friend and someone who could lighten up even the darkest day. The world lost an amazing talent and loving human being when you left us Pete. You remain an inspiration and your legacy will not be forgotten.

1. INTRODUCTION

"Imagination is more important than knowledge. For knowledge is limited, whereas imagination embraces the entire world, stimulating progress, giving birth to evolution"

Albert Einstein

For most people, the subject of pensions is not the most attractive of subjects despite, for many, it being their largest 'bank account'.

I am about to change that for you!

What if I told you that laying waiting to be found, in plain view, is a well-established, fully compliant, yet seldom talked about system that will enable YOU to actively take control of your pension strategy - no matter what age you are. Furthermore, it could have a profound effect on not just your pensions but bring enablement, connection, collaboration, passion and opportunity that is almost inconceivable to most - and all from a pension.

Residing deep within these pages is something very special indeed, something so special in fact that 99% of the population have not heard of it, let alone understand it – yet! Until this book that is!

It is also fully supported by the UK Government, has been around for over 40 years and is based on the oldest form of Law.

After reading and digesting this book you will be one of an elite few who are fully equipped and who understand this incredible game changing opportunity that awaits you.

You will gain the skills, knowledge and ability to unlock the power and to harness it, empowering you to enable a personal economy that delivers a wealth of fulfilling riches at every level of life, for you and your family.

The advantages for you will not only be potentially economically life changing, it will also engage a deep sense of satisfaction, control and knowledge that will calm any anxiety that you may have of never truly being in control of your personal economy - until now!

The secret that can be unlocked and harnessed is the wonderful world of SSAS pensions.

It is not part of elite Special Forces (SAS) or Software as a Service (SaaS)! They sound similar, however, this is very different, but it does have one common characteristic with both of these. In the right hands it can achieve amazing things!

It has the power to create a super-charging your personal economy and be a fundamental driving force behind your wealth creation strategy.

This is something far more impactful on your personal wealth creation and mindfulness. It will potentially be one of the most catalytic components for you, **CREATING EXTRAORDINARY LEVELS OF COMPOUNDING WEALTH.**

It will enable your personal economy to be fuelled with an unrivalled source of funds, freedom, opportunity and drive a very healthy thirst for education, knowledge and its responsible application.

I am guessing that you have never heard pensions referred to in this way before!

This detailed book is the first of its kind written and will blow the lid off this HMRC approved, previously almost unheard of and mysterious pension approach that could change your life in so many ways.

Whether you have a current pension or no pension at all, whether you are 15 years old or 60+ years old, there is value packed into this book that will serve you for decades to come.

This is the magic of SSAS.

I am going to take you through a journey of exactly what a SSAS is, how you can gain the knowledge, experience and skills that will enable you to consider a SSAS as a game changing part of your personal economy.

Being a Trustee of a SSAS will require tenacity, vision and application for sure. However, the transformative benefits run far beyond the compelling economic considerations into a deep understanding of what has previously been the last out-post of most people's personal economy, which to date, has probably remained an enigma!

That is about to change and here is your opportunity to crack that code!

The SSAS pension and the manner in which it can significantly change your outlook on life turns the arid subject of pensions into a vibrant, exhilarating and dynamic part of your life - and fun too!

Are you one of the 99% of the population whose pension strategy is to pay into a monthly scheme for 40-50 years, devoting 1-2 MINUTES each year to opening your annual pension statement, looking at it blankly, focusing on how it has grown, or shrunk, in the last year and hoping to goodness that it improves next year?

Don't be afraid to admit it as that was me for about a quarter of a century!

Yes, it would still hurt to think of that time IF I chose to look back on it, but I choose not to, I have now moved on.

Having made the decision to retire from corporate life in my mid-forties, to establish a number of new business ventures, it was incredibly important for me to use this pivotal point in my life to take control of every part of my personal economy. I had the privilege of spending much of my corporate life in massively changing economies such as telecommunications, data centres and energy and I was pretty sure that the only certainty in the future would be change.

Those that savour change, anticipate where the world is going and have the moral fortitude and courage to equip themselves with the skills, assets and structure to navigate these exponential macro economical shifts in the future, will be best able to identify and seize the opportunities that await. Those that do not may well be consigned to a life of reaction and servitude.

To enable a successful personal economy directly enabling a life of choice, freedom and opportunity, the following three core principles should become evergreen in your family plan and they sit right at the heart of a SSAS pension too. In fact, SSAS and personal economy work in concert with each other:

a. Create wealth

b. Preserve wealth

c. Multiply wealth

The 3 Pillars of Wealth

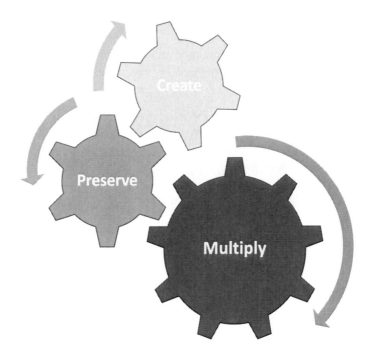

Being in my forties and having four children, my mind was turning towards the multi-generation aspect of our legacy and how we can equip our children with the very best assets, skills and opportunities to continue what we have started.

So that was the challenge I set myself!

For the last 26 years I had held various positions from Managing Director, Chairman and Non-Executive Director in national and international roles. However, despite being in executive positions with all the trappings of success such as stock options, shares and all the toys, I had always been an employee and that single reliance on any single organisation, event or person was about to come to an end.

Diversification, structure and resilience, whilst being hallmarks of our corporate services, were about to step up a gear in my personal economy also.

The search was on in all areas of my economy to create this ownership, control and security. As an employee for 26 years my focus soon turned to our pensions and considering what options I had. When I retired from corporate life in 2015 at the age of 45 years, I was still 10 years away from the recently announced age of 55 that individuals could access 25% of their pension in a tax-free lump sum.

In recent information revealed by a Freedom of Information Request, figures show that £23bn has been withdrawn under the 2015 government announced tax-free pension freedoms.

I felt deeply uncomfortable with having faceless pension managers charging fees for managing my wealth and so set myself the target of becoming an expert in my own personal economy – every single option and element.

It was not long before I came across the options of a SIPP or a SSAS. I will run through the fundamental differences later in this book but suffice to say that after some exhaustive investigation, I quickly settled on the merits and advantages of a Small Self-Administered Scheme (SSAS).

What I uncovered along the way was something incredible. I was able to follow a clear process to access one of the largest 'bank accounts' I had and turn this into a tax protected, highly efficient, deeply inspirational multi-generational wealth creation Trust many, many, years before I was even close to any of the definitions of retirement age.

Furthermore, I found a very small, yet growing community of people who had also 'voted out of the traditional pension system' and who shared my contrarian nature. They also had the courage, determination and endeavour to challenge tradition and seek a better life and outcome for their families and close friendship circles.

When you immerse yourself in the SSAS world you will find, as I have done, that we are not competing with each other; we are competing with what we are capable of. Once you truly understand this you will find an incredible rush of energy which is infectious and has the ability to create shared value to all those you come into contact with.

We have found this in our property development business, where we are the catalyst, the genesis, the curators and the custodians of enormous value creation and we genuinely care about everyone benefiting from a development. It is the essence of a truly sustainable business model.

The principles of Creating Shared Value (CSV) are the foundations of all our businesses and are a hugely important code of ethics for us. It is our culture, enshrined in our DNA and we are delighted that the SSAS Alliance community of like-minded SSAS Trustees has established a family of hugely talented people who appear to also live their lives on foundation values such as:

- Collaboration
- Independence
- Trust
- Connection

- Take control of personal economy
- Visionary
- Life of choice
- Ownership
- Driven
- Compliance
- Legacy
- Everyone wins
- Enjoyment

Another consistent trait across SSAS Trustees is a deeply personal connection between their values, their economy but also their why and purpose – what makes them leap out of bed in the morning enthused, refreshed and charged to achieve. Each of us have very different personal goals, targets and objectives in our lives - whether that is our time, our family, future generations or travel etc. Consistently those that have a very clear purpose and 'why' have been able to successfully encompass the wonderful world of SSAS Trusteeship into significantly advancing towards the realisation of their goals.

In his incredibly humbling book 'Man's Search for Meaning', Viktor Frankl said "He who has a why, can bear almost any how." The context of the book based on his experiences in Nazi concentration camps truly etches the meaning of these words in my mind.

We will study the Grosvenor Estate Trust model in this book. However, one of their recent statements lays clear their approach, which as SSAS Trustees and potential future Trustees, we may consider helpful:

"The reason that the Grosvenor Estate holds assets, via Trusts, is to ensure continuity of the collective ownership, administration and management of the estate across the generations.

This enables a far-sighted approach to be taken, ensuring a lasting commercial and social benefit is delivered from our activities. We are not driven by short-term considerations and this affords us a perspective that we believe to be in the interests of the Grosvenor family, employees and the communities in which we operate."

I know that reading or listening to this book can be that defining point in YOUR life. There was no practical, detailed and independent guide available when I started looking into SSAS – there is now, with this book, which I hope will enable you to learn from the knowledge I have researched, avoid the mistakes I have made, save time by making carefully considered decisions and rapidly fast tracking your understanding and engagement in this amazing opportunity.

I firmly believe this book will pay you a very handsome return on investment, probably one of the highest you will ever achieve. It is that powerful if you follow the right steps and start to excel at managing your personal economy.

This is where you can start your journey - understanding what a SSAS is, how you can become one of the growing community of people who are leading this change in their lives and bringing massive value to your pension, as well as shared value to many others around you.

I hope this book will become your invaluable companion for years to come and I want it to become that dog eared and well worn 'bible' on your desk, helping to navigate you along your hugely rewarding SSAS journey.

However, a SSAS is not for everyone - nothing ever is right for everyone, there is no 'one size fits all' in this field. If you recognise any of the following traits lying deep within your soul, then you will definitely become absorbed in the secrets and game changing strategies in the pages that lie ahead:

- Accountable

- Passionate

- Lead a life of choices
- Passion for controlling
- Tax efficiency
- Love collaboration
- Connecting with amazing people
- Love business

As we move into the detail I want you to imagine your life where you are in control of your pension - you make the decisions, you are responsible for your investments, you control the amount of time you apply to it, the type of risks you are comfortable with and the level of returns and growth you are happy with.

If this is ticking your boxes, the coming chapters are going to blow your mind with the world of possibilities and opportunities that are open to you.

My Wage

I bargained with Life for a penny,
And Life would pay no more,
However, I begged at evening
When I counted my scanty store;

For Life is a just employer,
He gives you what you ask,
But once you have set the wages,
Why, you must bear the task.

I worked for a menial's hire,
Only to learn, dismayed,
That any wage I had asked of Life,
Life would have paid.

Jessie B. Rittenhouse (1869 – 1948)

2. WHAT IS A SSAS PENSION

"Our favourite holding period is forever"

Warren Buffett

A Small Self-Administered Scheme (SSAS) is a pension Trust set up by a limited company or a partnership. A SSAS is primarily set up by private and family run limited companies for the benefit of the owner directors and senior employees. The members are also Trustees and so have control and flexibility over the Scheme assets and investment choices in a tax efficient environment.

The key features of a SSAS are:

- It is an occupational pension scheme
- The members are usually directors or employees of the sponsoring employer
- There is a limit of 11 members
- It is a highly tax efficient environment
- You have control of the investment decisions

A SSAS is an occupational pension scheme established in the Finance Act 1973 and is usually, but not always, set up by the directors of a business. The directors may want greater control over the investment decisions for their pensions, especially the use of their pension plans, to invest back into their business or indeed other businesses, should they wish.

A SSAS is registered with HMRC and so benefits from wide ranging and generous tax reliefs available to pension schemes. These may include, but not limited to:

- No Income Tax on allowable investments
- No Capital Gains Tax due on disposal of investments
- Company and personal contributions are deductible against tax
- Tax-free lump sum on death before retirement
- Tax-free lump sum from age 55 on retirement

A SSAS is not an FCA regulated product and so the 'wrapper' or vehicle is not covered by the Financial Services Compensation Scheme (FSCS). However, the FSCS does cover any regulated investments held by the SSAS.

Each member of the SSAS is a Trustee which is a requirement to comply with the Pensions Act 1995.

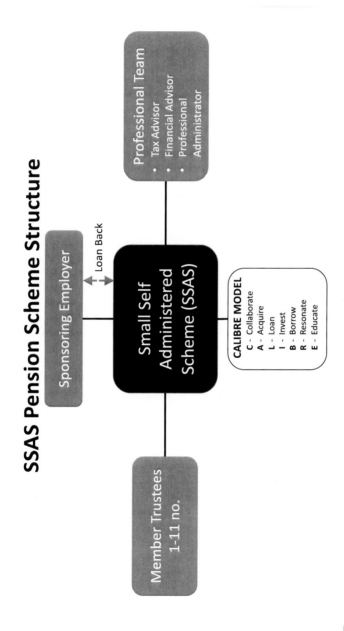

SSAS Pension Scheme Structure

Professional Team
- Tax Advisor
- Financial Advisor
- Professional Administrator

Sponsoring Employer

Loan Back

Small Self Administered Scheme (SSAS)

CALIBRE MODEL
- **C** - Collaborate
- **A** - Acquire
- **L** - Loan
- **I** - Invest
- **B** - Borrow
- **R** - Resonate
- **E** - Educate

Member Trustees 1-11 no.

A SSAS is a truly eye-opening concept that will leave you wondering why you didn't know about it long ago, irrespective of what age you are! And that can be a fear for many – they don't know what they don't know.

Being a Trustee of your own SSAS is similar in many respects to running your own business. In fact, it calls on exactly the same business acumen and tenacity and should not be something that should be feared. For sure, there are rules to learn and be followed, the same as in any walk of life. However, once you have mastered the basics relatively quickly you will start to see the immediate benefits and experienced the feeling of freedom and control which will, I assure you, become intoxicating!

The responsibility should not be taken lightly in setting up any business and a SSAS is no different in that respect. Embrace the knowledge and drive your own path towards an incredibly fulfilling future with the empowerment of a SSAS pension.

A key reason and driver behind the Pension Act 1995 was as a direct result of the unscrupulous actions of Robert Maxwell, who embezzled substantial funds from the pension fund of Mirror Group Newspapers.

On 5 November 1991, Maxwell was on his yacht, the Lady Ghislaine and during early morning his crew found him missing. Maxwell was presumed to have fallen overboard from the vessel, which was cruising off the Canary Islands, and his naked body was subsequently recovered from the Atlantic Ocean.

Maxwell's death triggered a flood of instability, with banks frantically calling in their massive loans. His sons, Kevin and Ian, struggled to hold the empire together but were unable to prevent its collapse. It emerged that, without adequate prior authorisation, Maxwell had used hundreds of millions of pounds from his group of company's pension funds to support the shares of the Mirror Group, to prevent bankruptcy. Eventually, the pension funds were replenished with monies from investment banks such as Lehman Brothers and Goldman Sachs, as well as the British government. Maxwell's theft of pension funds was partly repaid from public funds - the result was that pensioners received about 50% of their company pension entitlement.

Many of the features introduced by the Pensions Act 1995 in response to these national mechanism failures were later abolished or amended and refined by the Pensions Act 2004.

The Pension Regulator confirmed that at the 2018 year-end 22,070 SSAS schemes existed with 15,860 listed as having an external administrator which represents 71.9%.

This is not a widely understood or adopted pension strategy. However, it continues to increase dramatically, and this growth is predicted to become exponential as the benefits are better understood by people business experience and have the confidence and assurance in their own ability to run a SSAS scheme.

3. RETIREMENT & TRADITIONAL PENSIONS

**"From my very first day as an entrepreneur,
I've felt the only mission worth pursuing in business is
to make people's lives better"**

Richard Branson

It appears to me that society is conditioned into accepting that we have a preordained route in life. This starts very early from our visit to the careers office or the questions children are asked, such as "what do you want to be when you grow up?". The answer invariably being one of a form of employment in a pre-set structure. I am not saying there is anything wrong with that at all, in fact it is only right that we all have the freedom of choice to follow our head and our hearts into leading a fulfilling life. What I am saying is that the vast array of options of 'opting out' of the traditional way of life are generally left unheard, unacknowledged and unexplored by many until much later in life, if ever.

Life is fundamentally about choice. Anything that restricts, blinkers or suppresses the options available must be counter-productive to that aim.

We all have a different risk appetite that we are comfortable with. Have you ever thought about the risk of not doing anything and sticking with the norm? Well staying safe may not be as safe as you might think!

How safe is your traditional pension? Well certainly since the mid 1990's pension protection has increased beyond all recognition and indeed continues to evolve. However, the litany of pension scandals still taints the water, right through to recent times, and the question that I have asked myself - and maybe you should ask yourself - is how secure do I feel in having someone else manage my money and therefore a significant part of my future?

Let us have a look at some of the headline pension scandals over recent years which might give you cause to understand the alternatives in much more detail:

1. **Carillion** had a pension deficit of £580m. However, this is now likely to rise to over £800m because it no longer has a solvent business standing alongside it.

2. **Monarch Airline's** pension fund had to be rescued after a £158million deficit. The airline carrier eventually went into receivership in October 2018.

3. **National Bus Company**: As the National Bus Company was privatised in the 1980s, the Treasury removed £168 million from the company's pension scheme surplus. The official Pensions Ombudsman ruled in 1996 that the money had to be repaid.

4. **Tata Steel** who employee thousands of people in the UK is restructuring its £15bn pension scheme with uncertain consequences.

5. **Maersk and Sea-Land Services**: When Maersk acquired Sea-Land Services it initially stated it would not fund the deficit in the shipping firm's pension plan, which potentially left some of Sea-Land Services' UK members facing a loss of up to 50% of their future pensions. Maersk changed their minds, after a long period of very negative publicity, and decided to meet the full deficit of the pension plan meaning the scheme's 196 members would receive full retirement benefits.

6. **BHS** went into receivership in 2016 with a massive pension deficit, just a year after Taveta Investments, which is controlled by Sir Philip Green's family, had sold it for £1.

7. **Equitable Life**: One of the UK's leading private pension companies. The organisation closed its doors to new business in 2000 and then almost collapsed after reporting to policyholders over inflated valuations. Following High Court intervention, Equitable Life was not only forced to reduce the value of pension pots being accumulated by savers, but also to cut pensions already being paid to some of its customers. The government decided to compensate over 1.5 million of the policyholders for their 'relative loss as a consequence of regulatory failure.'

8. Changing the inflation mechanism: Instead of using the retail price index measure of inflation, the government has proposed to use the typically lower consumer price index. The move will affect the state pension and public sector pensions, as well as some private sector pensions. Pensioner groups have reacted angrily to the switch, which could wipe off about £100 billion from private sector pension liabilities alone.

9. **Robert Maxwell**: In 1991, following his death, the media tycoon was found to have stolen more than £400m from 32,000 company members of the Mirror Group pension scheme.

10. Other examples of huge uncertainty in corporate world regarding pension schemes include IAG, BT and BAE.

Failed pension schemes were bailed out with a record £661million by The Pension Protection Fund last year, with successful small companies footing a huge chunk of the bill. The Pension Protection Fund (TPPF) steps in to save schemes when they are facing collapse, meaning savers do not lose everything.

In the 12 months to March 2018, it paid out £661.3m to 129,661 pensioners which was an increase of £1.4million a decade ago when The Pension Protection Fund launched. These very significant pay-outs highlight the substantial burden that is being placed on government by organisations which go into receivership.

What other gremlins are lurking out there waiting to become headline stories and add to the mounting uncertainty in the pension markets and possibly creating another tsunami of volatility for your pension of the future?

Lane Clark & Peacock (LCP) released an interesting annual report on the status of the pension markets (Accounting for Pensions) and the 2017 summary gives some startling findings which may start you thinking about where you want to invest your valuable pension assets. Here is a summary of a few of them:

- FTSE 100 companies paid four times as much in dividends in 2016 as they did in contributions.

- 8 companies reduced the assumed life expectancy in their pension scheme.

- Pension liabilities could reduce by £30bn if those using RPI were able to switch to CPI.

- There are now no traditional final salary pensions for new recruits at FTSE 100 companies.

- There is a significant Defined Benefit (DB) 'vs' defined contribution (DC) savings gap with the amount required to provide for a typical DB pension being 55% of salary, compared to DC pensions at 3% of salary under auto-enrolment.

- Liabilities may be being overstated – adopting improved methods of setting accounting assumptions could reduce the combined accounting liability for FTSE 100 pensions by £25bn.

- Pension schemes continue to pose a very significant potential risk for certain companies.

The companies with the biggest deficits, according to the 2017 report, were Royal Dutch Shell, BP, BT and BAE Systems. The four FTSE 100 companies each had a deficit of more than £6bn in 2016.

BT Group disclosed pension liabilities of £60 billion in its March 2017 accounts, up from £50 billion a year earlier.

However, perhaps LCP's most damning finding was that FTSE 100 companies paid out four times as much in dividends in 2016 as they handed over in contributions to their defined-benefit schemes.

One of the key takeaways from this excellent report is actually a question which I would like to pose to you: are you comfortable with your pension being in the cross hairs of a company deciding on the Pension v Shareholders equation, when they are publicly traded entities?

What would you have to be doing daily in order for you to never use the word pension again?

Probably something you love with a passion, I am guessing. Most people spend the very best years of their life grinding out an existence and pursuing a traditional pension to serve them at the end of their working life.

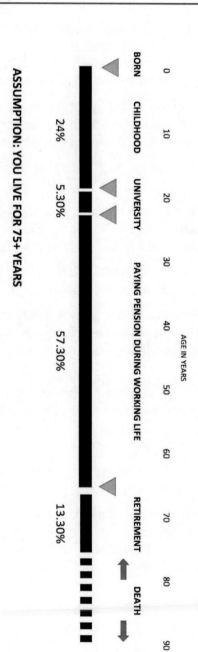

Life Span Events

Life Expectancy at Birth, UK, 1980 - 2037

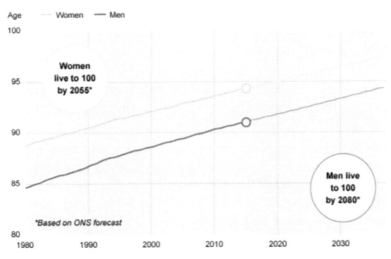

Source: Telegraph 15 Jan 2015

This image shows us the reality of what a traditional life tries to impose upon us. Based on a 75 year life span for someone going to university and then working until the age of 65 years would result in you having worked for 57.3% of your life to 'enjoy' 13.3% of your life in retirement.

It would make sense to have a very clear plan on your investments to ensure you have a clear strategy – in order to enable you to live a life that is fulfilling, rewarding and content.

Find something you love doing and build a business around it and immerse yourself in the options that enable you to live a fulfilling life of purpose and enjoyment. Many entrepreneurs enjoy their business activities that they may not choose to have a retirement point in their life. They may choose to scale back their time in business a little, possibly handing operational control to future generations but for many entrepreneurs it is what they love, it is what they do, and they receive a lot of fulfilment from having continued interests well beyond traditional retirement age.

Have you ever known someone who has retired, and the zest appears to disappear from their life? They seem to lose that point of reference, the context, the routine, the interaction and engagement and, in some cases, they may have passed away having never really lived the retirement life they had dreamed of and worked so hard to try to achieve.

The reality of a pension and what it will deliver to us is individual to each and every one of us. However, a brief look at the calculations on your pension pot and what it could mean to you is pretty disturbing news for most of society – and what is even more disturbing is that most people don't even realise what their pensions will provide them upon 'retirement'. In most cases it will simply not be sufficient to pay for the basic necessities in later life let alone an aspirational life of travel, fun and enjoyment.

Annuity rates used to be at 14%-16% in the 1990's, however currently languishing in the lower single digits we can no longer assume that what may have worked for our parents and previous generations will be suitable and appropriate to care for our futures

– unless you want to rely on the state or future volatile situations to affect our life.

When would you expect to retire – will it be men and women at an equitable age or state pension ages of 60 for women and 65 for men? Do you want anyone telling you when you will retire, or do you want to make that decision yourself? Think about that for a few minutes. Those that question tradition will see quickly that we have been conditioned to accept what society considers the norm. There is no reason why you cannot take matters into your own hands and define your own future. After all, an increasing number of people are doing just that.

Will future governments, with increased pressure on the state funds, be able to maintain current pension age levels or will this move to 70+ and beyond as the average lifespan increases?

A recent study by Dell Technologies stated that 85% of the jobs that will exist in 2030 have not even been invented yet!

By 2030 the number of US workers in full-time 'permanent' employment is forecast to drop to 9% of the workforce, an all-time low.

So in the ever changing world it is worth considering a few questions as you plan your longer term investment horizons and the risks that may exist:

- Is your pension secure and protected?
- Will your Final Salary Pension Scheme be around for you?
- Are you willing to take that risk?

Change is happening at an unprecedent level – will you anticipate change and take control or take your hands off the steering wheel, trust in faith and whomever you believe in and use words like:

- It was meant to be
- It was destiny
- We were unlucky
- Hope it will be better next year

Really?!

Is that the responsible attitude to pass down to your future generations? As Trustees we decided that was not the type of legacy we wished for our children and decided to change that with our SSAS implementation.

Here is a simple exercise for you to do on the readily available pension calculators:

PART 1: Run an example of your own circumstances on-line through www.moneyadviceservice.org.uk. I produced this example to illustrate the potential of your hard-earnt state pension.

- For Simon aged 49 with a salary of £30,000 per annum
- Current pension pot: £50,000

- His employee monthly pension contribution: £100
- Employer's monthly pension contribution: £100

By 2037 when Simon is 67 and reaches retirement age, his pension pot will be valued at £107,342 with a 25% tax free lump sum option of £26,835.

The ensuing weekly pension would be £164.35.

You will be able to compare this example to your current circumstances and decide how under or over stated this is for you. However, even at this level is that really going to give you the lifestyle you want or just contribute to some of your living and care costs?

PART 2: Add up your current lifestyle costs and project those to your lifestyle costs at retirement age. Remember to add any costs for the life you want to lead!

PART 3: Contact your pension company and ask for a transfer value for your current pension.

PART 4: Consider the options you have as you read or listen to this book on how that transfer value, transferred into a SSAS, might be deployed and the benefits, rewards, legacy and enjoyment it might provide with immediate effect through to retirement age, until you draw your last breath - and then beyond.

As you get to retirement age you can use your pension pot to buy an insurance policy that gives you a guaranteed income for the rest of your life. This is called an annuity and might include:

- Take 25% of your pot as tax-free cash and buy an annuity with the other 75%.
- A fixed income for life or for a set number of years.
- You pay tax on your annuity income.

If you are currently receiving a pension income, it's likely that you've already bought an annuity or are taking an income from your pension. Once you have made this decision the option to open a SSAS is probably not going to be possible, unless you have other pensions available.

Occupational pension schemes in the UK are usually defined by the type of benefit they provide. There are three main types:

- **Defined benefit schemes**: these are sometimes known as 'salary-related' or 'final salary' schemes.
- **Defined contribution schemes**: sometimes known as 'money purchase' schemes.
- **Hybrid schemes**: mixture of defined benefit and defined contribution benefits.

Each of these can be funded by contributions from the employer only (which is a 'non-contributory scheme') or from both the employer and employee (which is a 'contributory scheme').

There are other types of pension scheme in which employers can provide retirement benefits for their employees which include:

- Setting up a group personal pension scheme
- Offering a stakeholder pension scheme

How much income you get each year from an annuity depends on things like:

- How much you had in your pension pot when you bought the annuity
- Your age
- Whether you want the income to increase each year
- Whether you want the annuity to pay out to someone after you die
- Your health and lifestyle

It is worth stating that you will almost certainly have to pay administration fees on any annuity scheme.

Types of Annuity

Type	Methodology
Single life	Paid just to you, either for life or for a fixed number of years.
Joint life	Payments continue to your spouse or partner after you die.
Fixed term	Pays an income for a set number of years, then a guaranteed sum which you can invest or use to buy another annuity.
Short term	Stops paying at the end of a set number of years (up to 5 years) or when you die (whichever comes first).
Guaranteed period	Pays out for a set term even if you die within that term, e.g. you get a 10-year annuity and die after 7 years, your spouse or partner still gets payments for another 3 years or a lump sum.
Enhanced or Impaired	May pay more than a standard annuity if you smoke or have a medical condition e.g. diabetes or high blood pressure.
Escalating	The amount increases each year to reduce the effect of inflation.
Level	Pays a flat amount of income each year.
Investment linked	Tied to the stock market, the amount it pays can vary and depends on the success of the investments.
Capital protected	Your pot is paid to whomever you leave it to (your 'beneficiary') if you die within a set period, subject to tax.

Tax considerations: If you decide to buy an annuity you can still take up to 25% of your pension pot, tax free, as cash and this does not use up any of your Personal Allowance, which is the amount of income you don't pay tax on. With the remaining 75% you could then buy an annuity as an example.

You will pay tax on income from an annuity, just like you do on your salary, because when you are paying into your pension you get tax relief on your contributions.

If you take the 25% tax-free lump sum you must buy an annuity with the rest or use one of the other pension options.

The government website www.pensionwise.gov.uk provides an interesting source of high-level pension calculations that you can use as an alternative to others mentioned previously.

According to research by insurer Royal London in May 2018, you would need a pension pot of £260,000 if you wanted to avoid an uncomfortable retirement. This sum would provide a provide pension income of just over £9,000 in addition to the new state pension of £8,546.20 a year.

A final example of traditional pensions illustrates this table which compares a person retiring aged 55 years or 65 years and allows varying scenarios of taking tax free 25% sums at 55 years. Finally, it assesses a range of pension pots of £20,000, £50,000, £100,000 and £200,000.

For each scenario it provides a breakdown of the annual, monthly and weekly taxable pension income. It is a stark reminder of how so many people are blindly 'assuming' that their pension will look after them in later life. Could you live a rewarding life at 65 years with a pension pot of £50,000 equating to £40.38 per week to live on?

This should give us all serious food for thought if we would like to live something other than a life of servitude, when we should be enjoying our retirement!

RETIRE AT 55 years old		TAXABLE PENSION INCOME		
PENSION POT	TAX FREE AT 55	ANNUAL	MONTHLY	WEEKLY
£20,000.00	£5,000.00	£700.00	£58.33	£13.46
£50,000.00	£12,500.00	£1,600.00	£133.33	£30.77
£100,000.00	£25,000.00	£3,300.00	£275.00	£63.46
£200,000.00	£50,000.00	£6,600.00	£550.00	£126.92

RETIRE AT 65 years old		TAXABLE PENSION INCOME		
PENSION POT	TAX FREE AT 55	ANNUAL	MONTHLY	WEEKLY
£20,000.00	£5,000.00	£800.00	£66.67	£15.38
£50,000.00	£12,500.00	£2,100.00	£175.00	£40.38
£100,000.00	£25,000.00	£4,100.00	£341.67	£78.85
£200,000.00	£50,000.00	£8,200.00	£683.33	£157.69

Source: https://www.pensionwise.gov.uk/en/guaranteed-income

Note: Based on a single life non escalating annuity

4. SSAS V SIPP

**"The secret to success is to own nothing
but control everything"**

Nelson Rockefeller

One of the most frequent question that arises from those just hearing about a SSAS is whether it is similar to a SIPP and what the differences are.

A SIPP is a well-known and more widely adopted product and whilst having some areas in common, is structurally very different in some fundamental respects that must be understood in order for an informed decision to be made when choosing between them.

In summary, the key differences are that a SSAS:

- Has greater investment flexibility and control by the Trustees
- Funds are owned by the SSAS rather than allocated to a SIPP fund
- Can lend to the sponsoring company
- Has members that are Trustees
- Is a cost efficient pension scheme for company directors and/or other family members employed in the business

As a general rule, contributions made by your company (the sponsoring employer) will receive Corporation Tax relief. Personal pension contributions may also be made, and you could receive tax relief through self-assessment.

This initial tax relief is a key difference between a SSAS and other tax friendly savings, such as a SIPP or an Individual Savings Account (ISA). As your pension grows, the fund is largely free of tax and all the while you have control of the money you are investing.

Having your pension work for your business is the key difference between a SSAS and a SIPP. A SIPP will give you freedom to invest funds in a manner of your choosing, however it does not allow you to invest these funds back into the business by way of a commercial loan.

Before we can compare a SIPP and a SSAS let us take a look at what a SIPP is, to enable informed decision making and context.

SIPP

A Self-Invested Personal Pension (SIPP) is the name given to the type of UK government approved personal pension scheme, which allows individuals to make their own investment decisions from the full range of investments approved by HMRC.

SIPPs, like many personal pension schemes, are tax 'wrappers', allowing tax rebates on contributions in exchange for limitations on accessibility of funds. HMRC rules allow for a greater range of investments to be held within a SIPP than with other forms of personal pension schemes, notably equities and property and rules for contributions and benefit withdrawal are the same as for other personal pension schemes.

A SIPP is a personal pension plan set up by an insurance company or specialist SIPP operator, where the member has greater control over the investments. Anyone can take out a SIPP providing they meet the provider's eligibility requirements. These are usually based on a minimum fund size because of the higher costs involved in running a SIPP, compared to a standard personal pension.

Investors may make choices about what assets are bought, leased or sold, and decide when those assets are acquired or disposed of, subject to the agreement of the SIPP Trustees which are usually the SIPP provider itself. Joining a SIPP is open to anyone and is relatively straight forward to do. There are reasons why you might not choose a SIPP, but the rules don't limit who can have one.

All assets are permitted by HMRC, however some will be subject to tax charges. The assets that are not subject to a tax charge are:

- Stocks and shares listed on a recognised exchange
- Futures and options traded on a recognised futures exchange
- Authorised UK unit Trusts and open-ended investment companies
- Unauthorised unit Trusts that do not invest in residential property
- Unlisted shares
- Investment Trusts subject to FCA regulation

- Unitised insurance funds from EU insurers and IPAs
- Deposits and deposit interests
- Commercial property
- Ground rents excluding any element of residential property
- Traded endowments policies
- Derivatives products such as a contract for difference (CFD)
- Gold bullion provided it is 'investment grade'

Investments currently permitted by primary legislation but subsequently made subject to heavy tax penalties and therefore typically not allowed by most SIPP providers include:

- Any item of tangible movable property whose market value does not exceed £6,000
- 'Exotic' assets like vintage cars, wine, stamps, oriental rugs and art
- Residential property

A SIPP might have higher running costs, particularly if there is more than one member as each member has their own SIPP. Compare this with a SSAS, which can have up to 11 Trustees participating in the same fund with usually a singular cost base.

SSAS

Unlike a SIPP, a SSAS is classed as an occupational pension which means there are slightly different rules that govern it.

The pension scheme's assets are held in the name of the Trustees, but each member is viewed as having a share of these assets.

With a SSAS the small business and the members of the pension scheme can each make contributions to it.

One advantage for business owners is that a SSAS can invest in the directors' business and can lend money to their company, which a SIPP cannot do.

A SSAS is a small occupational pension scheme that is set up by the directors of a business that want more control over the investment decisions relating to their pensions and in particular, to use their pension plans to invest in the business. As such, each member of the SSAS is usually a Trustee.

This table lays out some of the comparisons between a SSAS and a SIPP which you may wish to consider and explore as part of your due diligence in deciding what is right for your personal circumstances:

SSAS	SIPP
Is an occupational pension scheme	Is a personal pension scheme
Trustees must have a sponsoring company and are usually limited to directors, employees and family members	Anyone can join
Can lend money to sponsoring employers	Loans are not allowed to any members or any person/ company connected to the member
Can invest up to 5% of the fund value in the shares of the sponsoring company	A SIPP doesn't have a sponsoring employer so can theoretically invest up to 100% of the fund in the shares of any company, including one run by the member
Can buy shares in more than one sponsoring employer so long as the total market value at the time the shares are bought, is less than 20% of the total value of the scheme	If the company involved is controlled by the SIPP member or an associated person, investment in that company would be regarded as investing in taxable property
SSAS can potentially own 100% of a company's shares so long as the value doesn't exceed 5% of the value of the SSAS	A SIPP can potentially own 100% of a company's shares so long as the company is not controlled by the member, and this is acceptable to the SIPP provider

As can be seen there are some key differences between the two. Ultimately, perhaps, the biggest difference for us is that a SSAS is particularly beneficial to company directors, hence a large proportion of business owners and directors are drawn towards a SSAS.

Membership of a SSAS requires a much higher degree of involvement in the administration of the scheme than a SIPP.

It is perfectly possible to transfer from a SIPP to a SSAS and I have seen this happen numerous times, particularly as the understanding of a SSAS is becoming more commonly known.

Deciding what is the right pension scheme for you should not be taken lightly. Your decision might bear in mind:

- What are your objectives?
- What strategy you are considering?
- Who the members are likely to be and your mutual relationship?
- To what level of involvement do you want in investment decisions?
- What are the costs?
- What level of control do you want?
- Personal preference?

When seeking independent advice when deciding whether a SIPP or a SSAS is right for you, ensure that the Independent Financial Advisor you choose is very knowledgeable and experienced in both of these. I have met a number of IFA's in the past who know a lot about SIPP's but relatively little about SSAS which provided little help in the process!

5. TRUST LAW

**"If everyone is thinking alike
then somebody isn't thinking"**

George S Patton

A Trust is a legal relationship created during a person's lifetime, or upon their death, when assets are placed under the control of a Trustee for the benefit of a beneficiary, or for a specified purpose.

A Trust has the following characteristics:

- A Trust is a separate legal entity in its own right
- Trust assets constitute a separate fund and are not a part of the Trustee's own personal estate
- Legal title to the Trust assets is in the name of the Trustee
- The Trustee has the power and the duty to manage, employ or dispose of the assets in accordance with the terms of the Trust and the special duties imposed by law

The key characteristic of a Trust is that it permits the separation of legal ownership and beneficial interest. The Trustees become the owners of the Trust property, as far as third parties are concerned, and the beneficiaries are entitled to expect that the Trustees will manage the Trust property for their benefit.

There are a number of types of Trust scenarios including:

Statutory Trust: Trust created by operation of law where a property is held by Trustees for immediate or eventual sale at their discretion. All income from the property prior to its sale, and all proceeds of its sale, are held in Trust for the benefit of the Trust's beneficiaries.

Resulting Trust: A type of Trust that is imposed by law. It returns the beneficial ownership in the Trust property back to the settlor. An example could be where the settlor of an Express Trust fails to tell the Trustees what to do with the Trust property.

For example, Stephen sets up a Discretionary Trust for the benefit of his siblings. However, he fails to say what will happen to the Trust once his siblings have died. Once his siblings die, and there are assets still held in Trust, the Trust assets are held on a resulting Trust for Stephen, or his estate, if Stephen has also died.

Implied Trust: Two types of implied Trusts are constructive and resulting Trusts. A resulting Trust arises from the conduct of the parties. A constructive Trust is an equitable remedy that enables plaintiffs to recover property, or damages, from defendants who would otherwise benefit inappropriately. An implied Trust arises by the operation of law. It is imposed by a legal process under law, to situations either by presuming an intention of the participants to create a Trust, or because of the facts at hand.

Grosvenor Estate

Grosvenor Estate is a well-known brand in property investment circles. However, what leapt to the general public's attention in 2016 was the death of the 6th Duke of Westminster, Gerald Cavendish at aged 64 and his succession by his son Hugh, to become the 7th Duke of Westminster.

The genesis of the Grosvenor family fortune date back more than 300 years when Sir Thomas Grosvenor married wealthy heiress Mary Davies. Mary Davies had inherited a medieval manor in Middlesex and 500 acres of land in West London which was undeveloped at the time.

The Grosvenor's then did something very special indeed all those centuries ago. They gave the land away to a Trust which we now know as the Grosvenor Estate. Since then it has enjoyed incredible tax privilege and benefits and the compounding effect of income, capital growth, astute investment and protection of the capital value has paid an extremely handsome return for one of the most famous Trusts in the world.

This land, which become a holding of the Grosvenor Estate, was developed in the early 1700's and became known as Mayfair. An additional parcel of land was later developed by the Grosvenor Family in the early 1800's and became known as Belgravia.

The Grosvenor Estate is purported to be valued at well in excess of £9 billion and comprises of property, a charitable foundation, a family office, the Wheatsheaf Group, as well as extensive investment portfolios.

Following speculation in the media surrounding Inheritance Tax, after the passing of the 6th Duke of Westminster, Grosvenor Estate issued a statement which provides interesting points for us to reflect on as SSAS Trustees. The statement reads:

"The business assets of the Grosvenor Estate are owned by a series of UK resident (i.e. onshore) Trusts, the beneficiaries of which are both current members of the Grosvenor family and future, as yet unborn, descendants. These assets consist of Grosvenor Group Limited, which manages, invests in and develops property in over 60 cities around the world; Wheatsheaf Group, which directly operates, invests in and helps to develop businesses in the food and agriculture sectors; and the Family Office, which manages the rural estates, other investments and the philanthropic activities, including the Westminster Foundation.

The reason that the Grosvenor Estate, like many other family owned enterprises, holds assets via Trusts is to ensure continuity of the collective ownership, administration and management of the estate across the generations.

This enables a far-sighted approach to be taken, ensuring a lasting commercial and social benefit is delivered from our activities. We are not driven by short-term considerations and this affords us a perspective that we believe to be in the interests of the Grosvenor family, employees and the communities in which we operate.

The UK resident Trusts are liable to pay income tax, capital gains tax and inheritance tax. Instead of a payment of 40% inheritance tax upon death, the majority of the Trusts are of a type that pay a rate of 6% every 10 years. This means that over a full lifetime, the Trusts will pay this tax many times over, with the added advantage to the UK taxpayer of its regular, effectively in-advance payment schedule. The remaining Trusts will be subject to 40% IHT on the death of the specific beneficiary.

As Grosvenor family members are all UK resident - and have been so for nearly 1,000 years - they pay UK taxes in the same way as the rest of us and are also entitled to the same exemptions.

Accordingly, and as one would expect, the assets left by the 6th Duke to his widow are exempt from inheritance tax. On her death, inheritance tax will be due in the usual manner."

The benefits of Trusts in general are that they do not form part of somebody's estate. In a discretionary Trust, Trustees have many potential strategies to consider for potential beneficiaries which the Trustees can choose to appoint benefits to, but no individual beneficiaries can demand money.

6. WHY A SSAS?

"Do not go where the path may lead, go instead where there is no path and leave a trail"

Ralph Waldo Emerson

In addition to the usual tax exemptions available for pension arrangements, a SSAS can offer other benefits for entrepreneurial business owners including:

- Purchasing commercial property to be leased back to your business (or third party).

- Loans to the sponsoring employer.

- Investing in your company by buying an equity stake.

- Transferring assets from you or your family, personally (known as 'in-specie' transfers).

Some clients prefer a SSAS as it allows some additional flexibility over other types of schemes, for example:

- The company can pay the scheme fees and offset the VAT.

- Pensions can be paid via the company's payroll rather than the pension provider's payroll which can save costs.

- Assets within the fund can be pooled (each member has a percentage of the total fund) or earmarked (specific assets are notionally allocated to specific members).

- Asset allocation can be changed from pooled to earmarked or the same in reverse.

- Company contributions have no direct link to salary so lower salaries can be drawn by the members to reduce income tax.

- Company contributions can be paid on an unallocated basis, so they are not specifically allocated to members until a later date. This has some planning opportunities.

- Executive pension policies can be assigned to a SSAS to boost its fund size for justifying loans, borrowing and company share purchases.

For some, the appeal of a SSAS is that they simply do not trust a traditional pension scheme and being 'pooled' with the masses.

For others they feel drawn to the 'safety' in numbers perceived comfort of doing what everyone else is doing. A SSAS is not for everyone as I mentioned before.

It is NOT for those that:

- Enjoy safety in numbers
- Want others to take their problem away from them
- Have little interest in growing their skills and education
- Cannot fulfil the criteria of setting up a SSAS
- Would not be able to act responsibly with fellow Trustees
- Procrastinates on decision making

A SSAS offers a completely ring-fenced stand-alone Trust with no co-mingling of funds. Funds do not form part of another company's balance sheet and have their own bank account. The SSAS members are Trustees and can be co-signatories on the bank account and joint registered holders of all investments.

For many, the appeal of a SSAS is something much more personal than just the tax efficient structure and economic benefits. It is about the 'greater than the sum of the parts' enablement which can materialise in so many areas such as:

- Great business acumen from previous business management experience
- The collaborative sense of being 'together' with fellow members
- Forming new relationships, extending old ones and having fun
- Extensive team support and leverage of their expertise
- As a collective SSAS you have more negotiation power
- As a collective SSAS you have more investment strength
- You are individuals as well as a Team
- You enjoy the benefits of the diversity and skills that the Trustees have
- The ability to apply the experience and skills to a wide array of investment options
- Having flexibility in your investment strategy

- Leaving a legacy and planning for the long-term
- Taking control of ALL of your personal economy
- Learning, connecting, controlling and collaborating
- Understanding the power, freedom and choice of a SSAS
- Being contrarian and opting out of the traditional pension system

I want to pose a simple question for you: What happens to your pensions when you die?

From a very close experience I have seen that the answer can be quite alarming. In one case my friend and business partner passed away suddenly in his early 50's.

The reality of his final salary and stakeholder pension provisions were that on death his wife, as his beneficiary, would receive circa 50% of the pension.

Only 50%!

A truly devastating financial loss compounding a tragic situation for a grieving family.

Where did the other 50% go I hear you ask?

Well who knows! However, it certainly did not make it to those that it was intended for, that is for certain.

On closer inspection, and to further highlight something equally troubling, should both husband and wife pass away at the same time, such as in a car accident, with some pension products the children would get nothing!

One of your first key questions is to ask your existing pension provider these two scenarios.

1. What proportion of my pension goes to my beneficiary if I die?

2. What proportion of my pension goes to my children if my beneficiary and I both die simultaneously?

Note: This assumes you are husband and wife intending to leave your estate to your children, however, the principle applies to any situation.

Let me know what the outcome is.

The irony is that my friend Pete was only weeks away from having his pension funds transferred into our SSAS pension. However, he sadly did not live to see that happen, nor did his family get to witness the protection that holding pension funds in a SSAS Trust environment has.

This was a desperately sad experience for all and one which I want to make sure you are 'eyes wide open' by asking the informed questions to really get under the skin of the fragility and risks possibly embedded within your current pensions. It will also enable you to take a considered and pragmatic view on their likely benefits of different scenarios, to take proper independent advice and to enable you to make a serious assessment of whether a SSAS pension is right for you.

On a positive note, I increasingly see fantastic relationships growing daily between SSAS Alliance members, who have funds to invest, and others that have a need for investor funds. This dynamic changes on a regular basis where the investor one month may become the seeker of investor funds a few months later – the relationships formed are truly inspirational.

Never has the law of reciprocity shone brighter!

In a recent poll the average SSAS Trustee's funds on a sample of over 120 Trustees was over £300,000 each. Bearing in mind that some SSAS's have multiple Trustees and you can see how the volume of investable funds in this sector is extremely substantial. With approaching 2,000 members that would equate to the SSAS Alliance membership having a collective £600,000,000 of funds under individual Trustee management.

Think of the endless possibilities that you could engage with if you had an inexhaustible supply of readily available capital!

Well, by creating great connections, working in a highly professional business manner and learning how to work effectively, transparently with each other, our great network can directly enable you to forge ahead and achieve anything you desire alongside like-minded and equally inspirational partners.

Irrespective of your view on retirement, there will come a time when you will want to slow down and spend your time in different ways.

How you decide now to build your wealth, create your asset base and define your strategy for risk management and long-term compounding returns, will directly reflect on your future net worth and being able to achieve your goals.

With a SSAS let us be very clear though – **YOU** are the money.

You have now entered into the wealth management business. To many this is a very liberating feeling and one that you should not be overawed by or take lightly but must quickly come to terms with the responsibility. Once the mind-set is right you can then enjoy enabling your Trust to deliver great value and satisfaction over many years to come.

7. NO PENSION? YOU STILL NEED TO KNOW SSAS!

"I've got too many of my friends that retired and went home and got on a rocking chair, and about a year and a half later, I'm always going to the cemetery"

Red Adair

"What is the point of understanding pensions when I don't have one", I hear you ask?

Well there can be many reasons. A very important reason is if you don't fully investigate and understand SSAS pensions you may be missing out on an incredible business or personal opportunity.

Let me explain what happened when we delivered a webinar specifically to SSAS Trustees in 2018.

Our development business works extensively with certified high net-worth individuals who invest in our various developments. Following numerous requests from Trustees on specific development investments we decided to offer an investment opportunity to a very selective group of pre-registered SSAS Trustees. This selective group had already been through extensive rigor and due diligence from HMRC for their SSAS establishment and approval, as well as their previous pension provider's, for funds transfer, as well as their SSAS administrator.

In the webinar, I presented an investment opportunity for a development in the South East of England and explained the overall opportunity, the risks, the reward, the structure and the time frames in a very transparent manner. In addition, I fielded open questions from attendees until we had exhaustively reviewed the opportunity over about a 2-hour period.

In the 24 hours that followed we received circa £2,000,000 of pledges to invest in the development.

This is a phenomenal rate and £900,000 of that £2,000,000 came in the first hour of the opportunity being opened.

The following weeks contained layers of bank grade due diligence by our legal team, the SSAS administrator and the SSAS Trustees until all parties were satisfied and the deal was completed.

This was an incredible moment after all the hard work, by so many people, to produce such a ground-breaking process enabling SSAS Trustees to invest in a substantial commercial property development opportunity. In addition to great returns, there is the opportunity to create incredible learning, to meet different people from different backgrounds and also enables a multi-faceted and diverse community.

This is a wonderful example of how a non SSAS related organisation with great people coming together with a shared vision can achieve great things collectively.

If you are looking for investment funds for your business and have done your homework and research and understand SSAS Trustees, their responsibilities, their strategy and are credible, then you may be able to offer a truly win:win opportunity.

Several of my roles in our various organisations include business strategy and investor relations. This is a wonderful role and affords me the distinct privilege of spending quality time with a wide range of successful business professionals from all walks of life. Some have created their businesses from scratch, later to sell them, whilst others have handed the business to the next generation through careful succession planning. Some have run organisations globally like I have, and others have concentrated on a specific asset class such as property, nationally. In summary, a very eclectic and diverse series of conversations from some incredibly intelligent, humble, driven and forward-thinking individuals.

Several traits that have emerged over the years from these conversations include the love of business, the tenacity of creating great shared value, the passion for identifying and negotiating a deal and the clarity of thought in knowing how their specific assets operate to serve their overarching goal.

The ability to be able to listen, ask questions, discuss and share counsel is something I consider a wonderful privilege and has led to many mutually rewarding and long-term relationships which are held with privilege and in confidence.

The power of collaboration with like-minded, yet individual people in their own right, has provided a richness of conversation that continues to directly enable shared and mutual value on a recurring basis.

I am sure the entrepreneurs amongst us have seen people endeavouring to borrow money or attract investment through social media without ever having undertaken due diligence and background research. It frankly communicates an unflattering elephant gun approach and rarely resonates with the more seasoned investor, let alone being remotely compliant with the Financial Conduct Authority Policy Statement 13/3.

Now compare that to a congruent conversation with a fellow business owner where you can have a confidential open disclosure of business interests and where you can both contribute something to the equation. If you are a SSAS Trustee, then you may well have funds to invest in the right opportunity as well as be interested in exploring their appetite to invest in your opportunity in another part of your business.

In any conversation you have with people, you may find that the most engaging conversations are the ones where useful information and learning happens. Where experiences, future plans, knowledge gained, and lessons learnt are openly exchanged and new solutions sought for the next opportunities. When both parties in a conversation are mentally stimulated, dynamically thinking and learning, then you have a very different and incredibly engaging formula that is working for everyone. I can assure you that these types of meetings rarely happen in isolation and a follow up meeting almost certainly arises.

Positive and successful people like to engage in positive and stimulating dialogue where opportunity abounds, Trust is built, and the creation of shared value sits at the heart of the outcome.

Whether you are a SSAS Trust or have no current pension provision, we all should have a come interest in tax compliance and efficiency. It is not exactly a dinner table conversation for most, but it is highly relevant and for those constructing long term compounding wealth it is critical in preserving wealth and accelerating exponential returns.

There is so much learning to be gained from the right qualified counsel and from those that are actually doing it!

A Chinese proverb says:

"Those who say it cannot be done, should not interrupt those doing it"

It may be that you can add significant value to your friends and acquaintances by letting them know of the power of a SSAS which could lead them to become more informed on the opportunities. If they then decided to proceed and establish a SSAS, they may be your future investors! That is lateral thinking of the creating shared value type.

Whilst you may not currently have a pension or it may be small, it may be that establishing a SSAS for all future contributions could be particularly appealing for you. This would need your due diligence, of course, and will depend on your age, your income, background and financial circumstances etc. None-the-less it could significantly enable the growth of your wealth.

I met a person recently who has maxed out on their Life Time Allowance for pension contributions, however another family member had used very little of this allowance and they have a number of companies between them. There is almost certainly a healthy discussion there, looking at their shareholding interests, dividends, income and savings and how best to optimise their personal economy - a SSAS may well fit into that planning.

You may have a protected pension such as those with blue light services (Police, Fire or Ambulance), NHS, MOD etc. For many this brings them up against a brick wall. For others they choose to ask how high the wall is to climb over, or how wide in order to go around!

It may be possible, with the correct knowledge and training, to have additional interests outside of your protective employment pension environment and establish property interests and then contribute additional pension contributions up to your annual allowance into a SSAS. This might be suitable for someone wanting to create some additional resilience by topping up contributions into a SSAS and outside of a protective pension.

A SSAS is one source of wealth and should you not have a SSAS it is certainly a very positive conversation that you could have on how best to collaborate with those that are SSAS Trustees.

This goes for any walk of life. If you can understand someone's circumstances and 'what great looks like to them' and possibly contribute to solving their problems, you will have a very engaging and rewarding relationship together!

Let us take an example of a person who is seeking increased income and has an unencumbered property - and therefore a first charge available. This may be of value to a SSAS Trustee who is considering a loan back (we explore this scenario in detail in this book in creating a win:win from value perceived by two parties).

Being a SSAS Trustee comes with much accountability and this is seldom taken lightly by Trustees. One of the incredibly humbling things I have experienced with the SSAS Alliance is the way our members almost self-police its content and membership. They want to work together in a collaborative and adult manner and there is an unwritten 'zero tolerance' attitude to those that disregard appropriateness, code of conduct, common courtesy, openness and humility.

Almost without exception, the operating of a SSAS is in addition to something else, whether that be employment, entrepreneurship or business etc and by understanding and getting to know Trustees one can really get to know people and their wider interests and passions.

Walking a mile in each other's shoes!!

In many respects the SSAS economy is an extension of a far great and more meaningful life study of the evolutionary journey to mastering one's person economy in its entirety. That makes the pillars of our wealth creation connected with the growth in ourselves, mastery of our expertise and disciplined in our long-term objectives.

Finally, and by no means least, it is a joy to meet interesting people who are passionate about collaboration and sharing. SSAS Trustees in the SSAS Alliance are amongst the most driven, engaging, convivial and dynamic people I have met.

They share a deep kindred spirit set in the responsibility and accountability of being a SSAS Trustee yet ignited by the passion of seizing control of the last remnant of their personal economy and embracing their control of their own destiny.

Why would you not want to immerse yourself in that type of positive culture with wonderful people?

8. BUSINESS BENEFITS OF HAVING A SSAS

"Shallow men believe in luck or in circumstance. Strong men believe in cause and effect"

Ralph Waldo Emerson

There are vast and valuable business benefits available to those with the tenacity to seek out and understand how a SSAS structure can support their business and personal aspirations and goals. It is one of the most potent forces that a business has at its disposal, that is seldom deployed given the very small proportion of SSAS pension schemes that currently exist.

This slow take up is starting to change and you are close to the 'tip of the arrow' in understanding this trail blazing strategy for your wealth accumulation.

Operating a SSAS is like running a business, there is no doubt about that. Understanding a SSAS should be of VERY significant interest to anyone running a business as there are some highly efficient and valuable benefits.

Before we look at the specific benefits, I want to highlight three simple phases of business including:

1. Start up

2. Growth

3. Exit

It is the last of these that I want you to pause for thought on. As a business person it is always wise to 'start with the end in mind'. Yet as many business owners will understand, one needs to be tenacious and agile to identify opportunity when it arises and seize it when it makes sense!

I frequently meet business men and women who have exited their business by selling through whatever means (trade sale, break up, merger etc) and many have taken important and wise steps to fully understand how a SSAS can best support them in optimising tax efficient outcomes as part of their business lifecycle.

Many of these previous business owners have received very significant sums of cash from the proceeds of a sale and consideration into how this is best structured can save tens, if not hundreds of thousands of pounds in unnecessary costs, including tax, which could have been handled in an alternative, yet fully compliant manner with a little forethought and consideration.

A summary of just some of the business benefits of having a SSAS include:

- Can reduce Corporation Tax every year as contributions are made
- Can receive a large pension contribution up to £500k and receive Corporation Tax relief in the current tax year
- Can receive carried forward pension contribution allowances of up to £120k per Director
- Company and personal contributions are deductible against tax
- Can receive pension contributions with or without cash from the business
- Can lend to the sponsoring employer
- Can buy your business premises
- Can borrow money to purchase commercial property
- Can receive rent tax free on commercial property
- Purchasing commercial property to be leased back to your business (or third party)
- No capital gains tax due on disposal of investments
- Can resolve auto enrolment issues for business owners
- Can hold all existing pension funds in one place under personal control
- Can reduce pension administration fees
- Can allow more flexible HMRC approved Investments than alternatives
- Can increase a pension fund through tax free and compound growth
- Trustees (business owners) can access 100% of the fund at age 55 (may not be tax efficient though above 25% though)
- A tax-free lump sum on death before retirement

- Investing in your company by buying an equity stake
- A tax-free lump sum from age 55 on retirement
- Transferring assets from you, or your family, personally ('in-specie' transfers)
- Provides business owners with control and efficiency
- No income tax on allowable investments

Historically, pensions were not popular with some business owners because:

- Lack of knowledge and awareness on the flexibility and enablement of SSAS
- They felt they could more effectively utilise any funds available for pension contributions within their own business
- The drawdown options at retirement were restrictive
- Annuity income levels were seen as derisory
- Putting cash into a Pension Scheme was seen as 'locking money away'
- Access to cash was paramount as bank lending was extremely limited

However, for those looking to create tax optimised and efficient businesses which work in concert with other interests, ignoring pension requirements is tantamount to missing out on massive opportunity.

Legislation is driving business owners to take more than a passing interest in pensions with it now mandatory that all businesses have the obligation to ensure their employees understand, and are made aware of, their entitlement to pensions through auto enrolment.

This increased awareness has been designed to ensure, as far as is possible, that all employees understand pension provision and planning for their future retirement options and that all employers take responsibility for their part. The government clearly has a vested interest in ensuring that in the future, today's employees do not become an unnecessary burden on the state. Whether this will translate into reality is unclear. However, for those willing to start the learning process, it certainly starts the thought process around long term wealth creation.

With this in mind, SSAS pension arrangements are an increasingly more understood option and an attractive proposition for all business owners as well as employees. The structure, agility, enablement and self-accountability of a SSAS often translates very readily to massive benefits to entrepreneurs and small to medium enterprise (SME).

Because a SSAS is a Trust, its assets are secured from creditors in other parts of your personal economy. This means, should a business experience financial hardship, the retirement fund of the SSAS would be safe.

Businesses without a SSAS in place will miss out on a smorgasbord of tax allowances and business benefits; those that have a SSAS in place, will be able to apply fundamental acceleration to many aspirations they have within their business, their pension and their personal environment.

In summary: A SSAS Pension, in the right hands can be a unique and lucrative long-term enabler in unlocking value and growth for businesses and their owners.

9. TYPES OF SSAS

**"Success is where preparation
and opportunity meet"**

Bobby Unser

There are a number of variations on the theme of SSAS structures, all of which will have different drivers and goals specific and unique to their Trustees' requirements. However, they will all share similar processes, governance and compliance, much of which is set out for you and illustrated in this book and in accordance with the core reference points such as HMRC, The Pension Regulator and good accounting practice.

Each of us are wired differently, we socially interact and engage at different levels, we have a hugely wide-ranging set of interests, skills and opinions and we connect with others in unique and varying levels.

One of my core corporate roles for over two decades in business was as a corporate trouble shooter, the Red Adair of the company if you like (for those of you who can remember this iconic global oil well firefighting expert from the US). Where any challenging issue or disastrous turn of events would need an immediate deployment and 'eyes and ears on the ground' to restore control and confidence, understand root cause analysis, establish leadership, to plan and execute a recovery plan, then invariably it was I that got the call to deploy.

Many of these situations were corporate issues that arose and once investigated I saw at first hand a consistent theme that had resulted in a complex series of events and control failures. That constant recurring theme was that of poorly constructed joint venture engagements.

Many of you reading or listening to this book may have business partners, joint venture partners through property, investing and other engagements. SSAS Trusteeship is another area where collaboration can result in parties pooling resources and coming together to create a 'greater than the sum of the parts' combined approach.

Whilst not wishing to poor cold water on the inspirational engagement of collaboration, after all this is something I believe in deeply, it MUST be accompanied with systematic due diligence and a good hard look in the mirror at one's self to really understand the key reasons for undertaking the venture. If everything passes muster then great, however do not miss this crucial phase.

Here are just some of my frequent findings from root cause analysis of fundamental joint venture failings:

- No alignment of values and objectives

- Roles not defined clearly

- Exits not clear

- Poor communication

- No formal agreement

- Key decision makers did not listen to their gut

- Those that had the idea did not have the skills to carry it out

- Lack of process and audit trail

Many a joint venture engagement has been dashed against the rocks after parties belatedly realised that their values, requirements, moral compass bearing, needs, styles and over philosophy were misaligned and incompatible. Unwinding any formal business engagement be it a Trust, Limited Company, Partnership etc is possible – however, it is time consuming, stressful and expensive and the opportunity cost of not proceeding with something else in the mean-time is often high. One other thing to consider is the often-lost opportunity of the business plan that you had joined forces to pursue in the first place!

If you decide to form a SSAS Trust with other parties, be aware of the potential pitfalls, undertake your due diligence, listen to your gut, be honest with yourself and others and then, and only then, proceed with a clear conscience into what I am sure will be a wonderful relationship as co-Trustees.

There are broadly 3 main types of SSAS as follows and we will take each one in turn:

Types of SSAS

Solo SSAS

1 trustee

Team SSAS

Typically 2-11 trustees

Family SSAS

Typically 2-11 trustees

Team SSAS

Some of the features of a Team SSAS (and also common with a Family SSAS) can include:

- You are part of a Team and that has a responsibility, a combined code of conduct and something intimate, engaging and bonding for all Trustee parties.

- You will have a 'joint and severally liable' relationship with each other and for the decisions you take together.

- There is support on hand from a wider range of skills and experience as a Team and you have the ability, in any given situation, to call on individual Trustee's specific skills and experience.

- As a collective SSAS Trust you may have substantially more negotiation capability and therefore strength, cohesion and resilience in your investment strategy.

- SSAS can be fun. This is an aspect that is often missed and the increasingly fun and engaging SSAS Alliance social events are testament to the benefits of being surrounded by like-minded and dynamic people who are celebrated for what they bring in terms of personal qualities as individuals.

- Some work best on their own, others feel lonely and prefer engagement, close company, a community feel, frequent counsel and to be on a journey to a common set of goals with others they respect.

Family SSAS

A family SSAS is pretty much what it says on the tin. It is a form of Team SSAS which typically may include members from the same family units such as husband, wife, parents, children etc.

- Some of the features of a family SSAS include:
- Existing relationships with known parties.
- Often contributing towards a readily agreeable family objective.
- Enjoyable family centric investment.
- Commonality points with a Team SSAS:
    o   joint and severally liable responsibility
    o   support from a wider range of skills and experience
    o   Substantial negotiation capability, strength, cohesion and resilience in your investment strategy
- Sharing of diversity of skills and experience to educate and grow connected family members through the SSAS.

Solo SSAS

A Solo SSAS is an individual becoming a Trustee of their own SSAS pension.

Many of the benefits we have discussed above in Team or Family SSAS's may not specifically apply within the Solo SSAS environment. However, the skills, relationships and business acumen that has been accrued over years of experience outside of any SSAS envelope will be equally valuable and can be applied liberally with the new-found knowledge of SSAS pensions.

A further significant advantage that many find extremely appealing with their SSAS pension is the value of interaction and collaboration with other SSAS pension Trusts.

This, above all, probably represents the one I get the most feedback from SSAS Trustees than any other. That priceless introduction, engagement and interaction between like-minded SSAS Trustees.

The encouragement, camaraderie and inspiration within an environment like the SSAS Alliance becomes a truly high-performance culture of driven and focused people loving the accessibility and learning and the transformation that SSAS has given them, as opposed to their often extremely dull co-existence with their previous pension vehicle!

10. YOUR FAMILY

"To enjoy good health, to bring true happiness to one's family, to bring peace to all, one must first discipline and control one's own mind.

If a man can control his mind, he can find the way to Enlightenment, and all wisdom and virtue will naturally come to him"

Buddha

When asking many friends in industry what their 'why' or goals are, one of the common elements that invariably is mentioned is that of a legacy.

The ability and desire to provide a legacy would be perfectly complemented and dare I say it, enhanced by the passion to create 'custodianship' to equip our younger generation to take on our life's work - and monumentally advance it for their future generations.

The SSAS pension is a multi-generational, highly tax efficient structure and is an asset which can be inherited and, therefore, kept within the family across generations.

That is why it is often referred to as a 'family pension'.

Let us harness the power of what has been provided for us and not squander it.

We are the custodians of an incredibly valuable baton and I firmly believe that we have an obligation to safely and securely hand that baton across to our future generations. I also believe we should do this well in advance of our dwindling years, enabling us to further bestow appropriate wisdom and counsel if called for and the enjoyment of witnessing the accelerated path our children will be taking.

The potent force of a SSAS is undeniable in the right hands and given that Trust Law is the oldest form of Law in the UK, will remain with us for generations to come. Many of us will be family members with a more than active interest in establishing an incredible legacy that will not only be left to future generations but will also be a nurturing incubator, enabling seeds of compounding that can enable something very special indeed to blossom over a very long term.

A SSAS can be a catalyst to a Multi-Generational Family Plan that will work actively in concert with other investments and income sources you may have, providing a balanced and long-term set of principles that will serve your future generations in a supportive and yet protective environment.

The core principles of the plan are in 5 parts:

1. Children
2. Custodianship
3. Education
4. Accountability
5. Legacy

Multi-Generational Family Plan

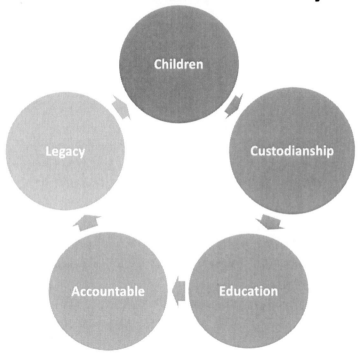

Whether your child starts their adult life via higher education, takes a gap year, goes directly into employment or immediately into entrepreneurship, each year that passes without storing and investing wealth delays the opportunity to enable the long-term massive advantages of compounding.

If I were to bring just one subject matter into the schooling curriculum it would be compounding and that is why the word figures so prominently in the title of this book.

The decision for young adults to become Trustees (you can become a Trustee at 18 years old) or to contribute to a stakeholder pension scheme with their first employer should be something that is given a lot of consideration and professional advice should be sought. However, do ensure that the advice that is sought is knowledgeable as well as independent and from an Independent Financial Advisor who actually knows and understands all of the options available, including a SSAS.

Take your mind back to the advice that you may have been given by your career's advisor at school. I don't recall anyone ever referring to entrepreneurship back then. You can encourage entrepreneurship in certain parts of your children's life from any age. It is the hunger, freedom, choice, tenacity and passion that fires the creative juices to learn and advance in life, whether this is done through employment or in less traditional entrepreneurial paths.

All have their merit if passion is ignited!

I believe this is one of the fundamental reasons why we, as more experienced adults with youngsters within our care - children, grandchildren, godchildren, nephews/nieces etc - have a duty of care to provide counsel, mentoring and support to them as they decide their first steps in planning for their futures.

If our legacy - their inheritance - is going to be partly in the form of a SSAS, then it would probably be best to equip them with a refined and powerful set of skills to manage this incredible opportunity.

11. OUR SSAS STORY

**"We are stubborn on vision.
We are flexible on details"**

Jeff Bezos

Over my my 26-year corporate career I had been a pension contributor since leaving Polytechnic. In reality, while I was a Chairman, Managing Director, Director or Non-Executive Director I was probably still in the 99% of the population who received their pension statements once a year, looked rather unimpressed at them for a few seconds and promptly hoped the performance might improve the next year – hardly an active participant in the day-to-day direction of one of my largest 'bank accounts'!

And that summarised my annual contribution to my pension management strategy for 26 years, outsourcing the pension contributions to my payroll colleagues and the 'active' management to a number of stakeholder/final salary pension scheme providers, who probably charged me substantial fees for the privilege.

The decision to retire from corporate life while still in my mid-40s was enshrined on the principle of wanting to spend more time with my family and friends, to live life on my own terms and to build a multi-generational legacy for my children, based on solid principles of entrepreneurship.

The final 'severing of the umbilical cord' of corporate life was to consider my options on my pensions that I had accumulated over the years. I was no longer happy to allow others to dictate and control my wealth and direction, hence I set about considering the options available for taking control of my pensions in their entirety!

After a short period of fact finding, research and deliberation it quickly became clear that the unregulated SSAS route allowed me the flexibility, control and accountability that I craved in my quest for financial independence and security – and in creating my own personal economy, particularly on a multi-generational basis.

Once the decision was made to go forward with a transfer we moved rapidly into the set-up and transfer phase – how hard could that be? Apparently you 'can't have a baby without the labour pains' springs to mind (I am reliably informed by my wife Sharon who has been there four times!) and so it turned out!

Our submission to HMRC was held up in a random audit which

delayed things by seven months and the transfer process took longer than anticipated due to highly uncooperative pension providers. However, with constant monitoring and chasing we finally got there and eventually my wife and I, along with two great friends Nigel and Annette, became fellow Trustees of our very own SSAS pension scheme – a very proud moment after all that effort. However, it was the sense of freedom and control from the corporate machine and now controlling a hugely powerful multi-generational wealth creation vehicle that provided the most satisfaction for us.

I shared with you earlier in the book how, as I was exiting corporate life and contemplating the next steps in our long-term pension strategy, friends Nigel Greene and Peter Abbott, along with their wives, were also contemplating this strategy too and we ultimately decided to become Trustees together in our own SSAS – a Team SSAS.

Within a year of leaving corporate life and while still in his early 50s, Pete sadly passed away from a heart attack leaving his wife and three children, the youngest of whom was only two years old at the time. His passing left everyone devastated. In what was meant to be a defining and exhilarating time in his life, fate cruelly denied Pete and his loved ones that joy, leaving a void that will be eternal.

Pete's set-up process and pension transfer had not completed into the newly formed SSAS at the time of his passing and with devastatingly clinical beauracracy, his life-long pension fund value was reduced on his passing by circa 50%.

Once pensions have been transferred into a SSAS, however, they are protected from inheritance tax and the Trusteeship can be transferred to the next generation.

This now forms a very important criterion for our SSAS moving forward. Not only does it create a wealth legacy for future generations but also enables us to nurture the custodianship of that legacy in our youngsters - Young Entrepreneurship live in action!

Pete taught me many things in the two decades that we were the best of friends and true to his most generous form, Pete continued to share and guide after his passing.

And so the plans for our SSAS? Well it will be no surprise to those that know Nigel and I that these plans are significant, long term and will establish a bow wave of great value through serious compounding over many years to come.

Several key aspects include:

- To enable our SSAS philosophy to become part of our foundation learning platform for our family of young entrepreneurs – a true incubator of talent and nurturing of business acumen.

- To establish a large portfolio of high-yielding commercial property assets.

- In creating commercial assets, establish further opportunities for adding value through conversions and enhancements.

- Use leverage to grow the Fund value exponentially over many years.

- Become 'black belts' in the Trust's management, opportunity seeking, value creation and risk management, compliance and governance associated with being a Trustee.

- Forge strong collaboration and synergy with other Trustees and developers.

As these objectives demonstrate, our approach will certainly be an active one which will serve our strategic goals admirably. However, it is important for me to explain how this relates to our Time – our most precious commodity.

It would be true to say that being a Trustee could be a full-time role if you wanted it to be. Our Trust sits harmoniously and synergistically with our other business interests and the adage of 'work hard to create the asset and then let the asset work hard for you' could not be more appropriate for our SSAS. We are clear that preservation of our time is paramount and hence we are carefully selecting assets which enable us to create an active engagement with minimal time required in the future.

This would equally be true for our SSAS funding which will include:

- Cash purchases
- Loan backs
- Business loans
- Bank leverage
- Other SSAS collaboration

Our desired funding will take into account the risk versus reward dynamics of what funding is required, how it is optimised and when it is engaged.

A good example of this would be the funding of a commercial to residential development. A SSAS cannot own residential assets, hence developing a conversion to residential scheme would require selling the end product prior to it becoming residential through its certificate of habitation.

In effect this requires selling and financing an incomplete asset, which creates a number of concerns and complexities for funders – and for us as developers it creates risk and uncertainty.

So what is our approach?

We are fairly conservative and not arbitrary risk takers, choosing to select routes based on assured outcomes where possible. We prefer to undertake any conversion scheme in its own SPV if the strategy is to develop and sell and possibly develop in a property company (often referred to as a Prop Co) if the strategy is to hold, depending on the asset class mix.

12. GROUND BREAKING RESEARCH: SSAS ALLIANCE SURVEY

"Too often we enjoy the comfort of opinion without the discomfort of thought"

John F. Kennedy

In 2018 we set an ambitious target to record data from the SSAS Alliance community and monitor on an annual basis some of the following:

1. How SSAS was perceived

2. What aspirations Trustees had

3. What their diversity of investment strategy was

4. The type of questions people new to SSAS were asking

5. How best we could help

We used Survey Monkey to invite SSAS Alliance members to take part and contribute towards a better understanding of how our community can improve and understand the challenges, the support and the solutions that can enable Trustees and those taking their first steps.

The response to the survey was emphatic – this was exactly what Trustees wanted.

After all we are only competing with what we are capable of!! Any tangible independently derived data that can support better understanding and decision-making, was welcomed with open arms.

The SSAS Alliance annual survey was born and over the years we will be tracking trends to help YOU gain evolutionary learning, to better enable and equip your SSAS and overall wealth strategy and access invaluable feedback that can help your SSAS direction.

In the following graphs you will see data on just a few of the questions that were posed in the 2018 SSAS Alliance Survey.

For a more comprehensive and up to date view of the findings, visit www.SSASalliance.org.

Some of the highlights from the survey include:

- Trustees have an average of £308,959 in SSAS funds
- Trusts have an average of two SSAS Trustees
- 39% are not sure what can be done with their SSAS

- 41% are unclear on a strategy for their SSAS fund
- 49% are unclear on how to deploy their SSAS funds
- 55% struggle to find trusted partners for their SSAS funds
- 43% find due diligence a challenge
- 17% are considering using their SSAS to invest in funds
- 8% are considering using their SSAS to invest in exchange traded funds
- 7% are considering using their SSAS to invest in trading stocks and shares
- 5% are considering using their SSAS to invest in commodities
- 36% are considering using their SSAS to invest in crowd funding
- 66% are considering using their SSAS to invest in their own projects
- 71% are considering using their SSAS to invest in commercial property
- 75% are considering using their SSAS to invest in commercial to residential conversion projects.
- 17% are considering using their SSAS to invest in hotels
- 15% are considering using their SSAS to invest in care homes
- 73% are considering using their SSAS to loan back to their business
- 70% are considering using their SSAS to loan to property professionals
- 70% are considering using their SSAS to collaborate with other SSAS owners
- 20% do not know if they are eligible for a SSAS
- 20% cannot decide between a solo or team SSAS
- 17% do not know the difference between a SIPP and a SSAS
- 21% wonder if their pension pot is too small for a SSAS

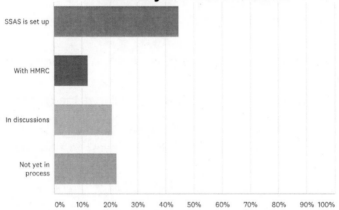

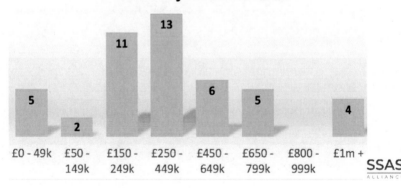

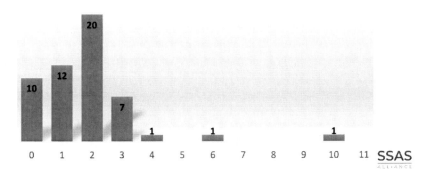

2018 SSAS Alliance Survey Results:
How many SSAS Trustees do you have?

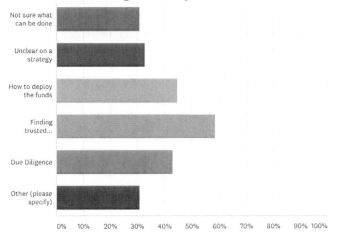

2018 SSAS Alliance Survey Results:
Challenges for your SSAS?

2018 SSAS Alliance Survey Results:
What are you considering doing with your funds?

ANSWER CHOICES	RESPONSES
▼ Investing in - Funds	12.07%
▼ Investing in - Exchange Traded funds	5.17%
▼ Investing in - Trading Stocks and Shares	6.90%
▼ Investing in - Commodities	6.90%
▼ Investing in - Alternatives	5.17%
▼ Investing in - Crowd Funding	27.59%
▼ Investing in - Own projects	70.69%
▼ Property - Commercial property	75.86%
▼ Property - Commercial to residential	77.59%
▼ Property - Hotels	18.97%
▼ Property - Care Homes	13.79%
▼ Property - Loan back to your business	77.59%
▼ Loans - Lending to property professionals	75.86%
▼ Loans - Collaborating with other SSAS owners	74.14%

2018 SSAS Alliance Survey Results:
Getting started? What are your key questions?

ANSWER CHOICES	RESPONSES
▼ Will I be eligible?	29.41%
▼ Advice needed on a final salary pension	11.76%
▼ Deciding between a solo /team SSAS	26.47%
▼ Differences between a SIPP and a SSAS	20.59%
▼ Is my pension pot too small?	23.53%
▼ Don't yet have a Limited company	2.94%

SSAS
ALLIANCE

Opinion is always readily available, specific feedback is interesting - however data is valuable!

As our membership grows from its current level to our forecast of 50,000 members over the next two years, the data set will advance dramatically and become increasingly more statistically relevant and accurate.

I look forward to sharing this progress regularly with you, in the years to come, at our SSAS Alliance Business Network regional events and at www.SSASalliance.org.

13. YOUR TIME

"How did it get so late so soon?"

Dr. Seuss

A Chinese fable recounts how a Zen Master gathers his students together and places in front of them a large clay pot. He then asks them to gather large rocks from the local area and fill the pot. They fill the pot to the brim and tell the Zen Master when they have completed the task. He asks them if the clay pot is full and they tell them it is.

The Zen Master then asks them to gather small stones and place them in the clay pot and once again the students gather stones and place them in between the large rocks in the clay pot. They return to the Zen Master who asks them if the clay pot is full. They inform him that it is.

The Zen Master then asks them to gather sand and pour into the clay pot. They pour in the sand and are surprised how much sand trickles between the stones and rocks and once it is full, they return to the Zen Master who asks if the clay pot is full. They confirm that it is.

The Zen Master then sits his students down around him and explains how this exercise is similar to the priorities in life. The rocks represent the important things in life which are top priority, the stones the less important things of medium priority and the sand of a low priority.

The clay pot represents your time in life he continues. If you fill your life with sand and stones, you will never be able to fit in the rocks. Prioritise the important things in life and do them first before allowing other things to take up your valuable time.

Sage wisdom indeed which is as relevant today as it was all those centuries ago.

I know many SSAS Trustees and I have yet to meet a single one that wanted to gain a full-time job of managing their SSAS pension once it had been approved and set up!

In fact, many share the desire that a SSAS will be a direct enabler to allow them to leave their employment at some stage in the future. I also understand that many people love their employment, however may want to enable themselves to have a life of choice, to do the job solely because they love it with a passion, rather than it being a financial necessity also.

Given that time is our most precious commodity, most of us that have been through the process of onboarding a SSAS are acutely aware, that in previous years, our pension management strategy and tactics amounted to a matter of a few minutes, hours or days each year. The decision to operate a SSAS seldom changes that conscious respect for one's time.

As we develop our strategies, we must be extremely conscious of our most valuable key performance indicator (KPI), our Return on Time Employed (RoTE), to ensure we do not unintentionally commit to vast swathes of time for little long-term return and creating a time drain, thus denying ourselves what we possibly set out to achieve in the first place!

The investment strategies available under HMRC guidelines to SSAS Trustees are many, flexible and varied and covered in a later chapter of this book. Each one has a very different time and frequency review period to it and you should be aware of this before embarking on each investment opportunity.

Your age will be an interesting factor in many of the decisions you choose to make. Some considerations may include:

Length of time to build up your pension pot through compounding: Some wish to directly grow their pension fund through long term gradual incremental increases, whilst others prefer a 'staircase' approach where large uplifts occur on a semi frequent basis possibly through property development or business investment. Your age and retirement plans will adapt to these variables.

Lower risk strategy: If you are older, you may choose to invest in a more cautious manner as any losses or negative positions experienced will mean you possibly have less time to recover until your funds are needed for your choice of retirement strategy.

Higher risk strategy: For younger SSAS Trustees they may find themselves drawn towards a higher risk, higher return set of investments looking to expand their pension fund rapidly and thus take advantage of the maximum number of years of high return compounding. Their considered view may be that should one of the investments experience a loss, whilst not ideal, they still have plenty of time to recover their position.

I was recently discussing with an ex-fund manager about this exact position and his views from years of high-profile management of significant funds. One of the worst-case scenarios was someone in later years recognising a compelling need to grow their fund value sharply to meet targets, thus moving towards a high-risk strategy with only a short term left until retirement and then experiencing the downside of high-risk investment strategies. This position has sadly occurred to many times leaving significant distress for those effected as they move towards retirement.

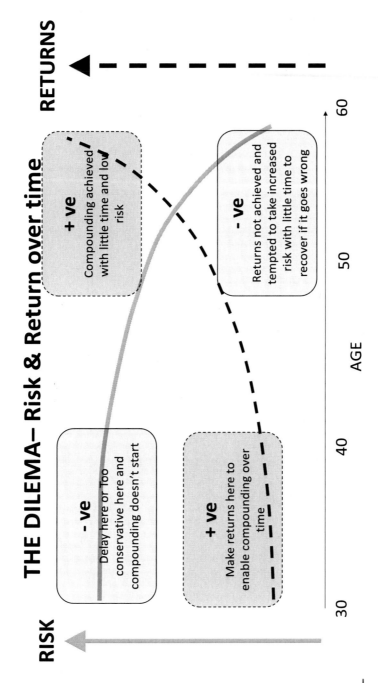

THE DILEMA– Risk & Return over time

RETURNS

RISK

+ ve
Compounding achieved with little time and low risk

- ve
Returns not achieved and tempted to take increased risk with little time to recover if it goes wrong

- ve
Delay here or Too conservative here and compounding doesn't start

+ ve
Make returns here to enable compounding over time

AGE

30   40   50   60

The younger generation just starting their adult life: We will consider this later in the 'family and children' part of this book. However, it is important that our children understand the benefits of a long-term compounding life-time pension strategy very early in life.

Children of today are rapidly moving into adulthood at a time of unprecedented change and opportunity. No longer are most markets local but now global in almost every sense. There is an immediacy of expectation in everything.

- To wait longer than 1-2 days for something to arrive in the post would be a tragedy!

- No WI-FI is disastrous.

- Societies ability to read lengthy text is reducing rapidly with sound bites seemingly taking over the world.

- Battery life is now a critical dependency.

- Saving to buy something is becoming increasingly archaic.

- More and more goods are leased rather than bought – mobile phones, cars, software as a service (SaaS - not to be confused with our core subject here!!)

- Connectivity of everything, through the Internet of Things (IoT)

- Cashless society where credit cards may become obsolete for increasingly large purchases with smart phones and wearable technology, such as smart watches, becoming your 'wallet'.

With these new skills that are being learnt there is an increased opportunity to monetise this and with more and more children understanding that jobs are not for life anymore, they are seeking diverse array of income streams and an entrepreneurial lifestyle. With these rewards under a business wrapper, very early on in life, tax efficient consideration, compounding and opportunity exist in abundance.

I know of one entrepreneur in his mid-twenties who has significant seven figure cash reserves and high-income levels from the sale of two businesses and the on-going running of a third. With the possibilities of the General Unallocated Fund and the diversity across our CALIBRE© model, both discussed later in this book, the range of tax optimised investment opportunity is there to be grasped if, and only if, the knowledge and expertise can be sought and embraced.

A SSAS could well offer very significant opportunities for this growing cohort of young entrepreneurs who are welcoming and embracing the lifestyle of choice, agility and control.

14. MENTAL STRENGTH & RESOLVE

"Never bend your head.
Always hold it high.
Look the world straight in the eye"

Helen Keller

No one ever said life would be easy - unless you went on that course, remember, you know the type, now what was it called? Ah yes, the "7 steps to a £million in a month"!!!

We all understand that there will be challenges along any chosen route, twists and turns and obstacles to overcome.

As an entrepreneur in taking onboard any new venture the emotion usually runs high, the enthusiasm drives us forward and the excitement mounts. For some, in fact for most of us, from time to time along the journey we should be humble to admit that this drive can occasionally wane. There's nothing harmful in admitting it, in fact quite the opposite: acknowledge it, anticipate it, prepare for it and embrace it as actually an opportunity to pause for thought, recalibrate, draw breath and move forward towards your lofty goal.

What better way to experience this than by surrounding yourself with incredible people in a great community, all coming from diverse business and life backgrounds, yet all sharing a common ethos of inspirational SSAS connection and collaboration.

The courage and mental strength you will need in your journey is going to be a powerful suite of habits, skills and mind-set that will serve you well in the years ahead and play a crucial part of the legacy you pass to future generations.

The following are a list of some of the things that courageous and mentally strong people have common traits of. They are not mutually exclusive nor are they definitive, however when I look at the experiences I have had and the successful people 'I have met over the years', whether they are SSAS Trustees or not, I can certainly recognise many of these attributes:

- They recognise that it is important to fail and are willing to do so as part of life's evolution.
- They understand and regularly evaluate their core beliefs.
- They enjoy spending time thinking on their own. They are comfortable with their own company.
- They love and embrace the change and enjoy identifying and seizing on new opportunities.

- They are prepared to be outside of their comfort zone and to experience discomfort to achieve a larger outcome.

- They move on rapidly. They are focused on now and the future and do not get lost in the past. They do, however, learn lessons from past experiences.

- They are passionate about maintaining control of the things they value highly.

- They have determination and play the long game.

- They are prepared to be highly personally accountable.

- They thrive on learning and expanding their minds.

- They will set clear goals and objectives and regularly consider the progress they have made - and change course if necessary.

- They surround themselves with inspirational and positive people.

- They enjoy celebrating the success of others, as well as their own success.

- They understand risk, identify how to manage it and enjoy the challenge of taking measured risk for enhanced returns.

- They hold themselves fully accountable and act accordingly.

- They thrive on efficiency and productivity.

- They detest waste.

- The love a challenge that will expand their thinking, connection and rewards.

15. STRATEGY

**"An investor without investment objectives
is like a traveller without a destination"**

Anonymous

Strategy is essentially the means by which an organisation aims to achieve its objectives.

Strategic planning is a systematic process that helps you set an ambition for your SSAS Trust's future and determines how best to achieve it.

Its primary purpose is to connect three key areas:

- Your mission - defining your business purpose

- Your vision - describing what you want to achieve

- Your plan - outlining how you want to achieve your ultimate goals

Strategic planning is different to business planning and requires stepping back from your day-to-day operations and articulating where your business is heading, by setting long-term goals, objectives and priorities for the future. In many respects one needs to do this within the SSAS itself but also thinking multi dimensionally, as the SSAS plays a core part of your strategic platform for your personal economy – it may indeed be a core component of your long-term strategic plan.

The importance of strategic planning cannot be underestimated - it is necessary to determine the direction of, not only your SSAS, but all your business interests to enable them to work effectively in concert with each other – with you being the conductor. It focuses your efforts and ensures that common goals remain in sharp focus. It may also help you:

- Agree actions that will enable business growth

- Optimising resources

- Prioritise financial needs

- Build competitive advantage

- Manage risk

Risk

Risk sits right at the heart of our strategic thinking and operational execution. In the chapter on Your Time we refer to your age and its relationship to your risk appetite. The older you are, depending on your financial circumstances, the less risk you may decide to take given that you have less time to recover in the event of a loss occurring.

Each Trust and indeed Trustee may have a differing approach to risk. As a board of Trustees, you will have to reconcile your Statement of Investment Principles with your agreed risk profile.

The Risk Tolerance Scale assesses the impact of the level of risk with the appetite for investment from conservative to aggressive level and the corresponding level of returns, both positive and negative of course.

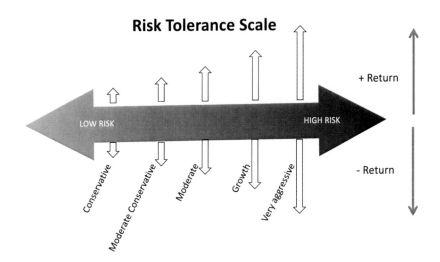

Statement of Investment Principles

An important document for you to consider, create and review with your fellow Trustees is a Statement of Investment Principles (SoIP). This will enable you to clearly document what your strategy is, and why, and enshrine the plan for achieving your jointly agreed goals.

A robust SoIP may include the following areas:

- Introduction
- Governance
- Investment objectives
- Investment beliefs
- Delivering the investment objectives
- Day to day operations
- Responsible investments
- Communication, reporting and transparency
- Compliance with this SoIP
- Appendices

Statement of Investment Principles

We will take each one of these in turn to provide an example of a deep framework for you to follow in your SSAS strategic planning with your fellow Trustees.

Introduction

This should briefly describe your purpose for creating this document including why it was created, who it is for, how it will be used and when you will review it.

Governance of the SSAS

There will be a number of statutory elements you will be required to comply with, such as HMRC. However, you will probably wish to add your own more specific set of rules to enable your Trust to operate effectively - to the satisfaction of all Trustees and interested parties. Some of these elements will include:

- Delegated authorities of the Trustees
- Day to day management of the SSAS's assets
- Investment Committee
- Type of investment strategy and assets
- HMRC mandatory reporting

Investment objectives

The Trustees must decide what their objectives will be under the SSAS. This will take into account all members and their specific requirements and expectations.

Likely considerations may include the following:

- Risk profile
- Risk management
- Returns

- Diversifications

- Budget and cost control

- Timescales

- Cashflow and reserves

- Compliance

- Exit and realisation of value

Investment beliefs

The Trustee sets out their investment beliefs to provide a transparent framework for consistent decision making. These beliefs act as a guide to enable effective delivery of all investment functions.

The Trustee's investment beliefs may consider:

- Understanding all Trustees' personalities, circumstances and attitudes is essential to developing and maintaining an appropriate investment strategy.

- As long-term investors, incorporating Environmental, Social and Governance (ESG) factors may be a consideration for you

- Deciding on the level and timing of investment risk

- Diversification approach when managing risk

- Monitoring asset values, economic conditions and long-term market developments thus enhancing long-term performance and informing strategic decisions

- Deciding on a blend of indexed management with active management

- Good governance

Delivering the investment objective

There will be many differing strategies that your SSAS Trust may adopt and this must be a decision that the Trustees come to an agreement on. Each decision must be understood in context with the resources available to the Trust. One of the major considerations here will be the time and expertise that you have available to deploy your investment objectives.

As Trustees you may not have, or wish to apply, the time required to manage each investment element of your strategy. This must be understood and reflected in your execution and deployment tactics and depending on the chosen route, could have an effect on your cost base and investment returns.

Investment risk management framework

To establish a best practice risk management framework, the Trustee should consider identifying four high-level guiding principles:

- Identify the most significant risk factors and rate them according to the impact they are expected to have on investment performance.

- Understand risks both individually and holistically.

- Identify available risk management tools and options – a useful start might be a risk register, per asset class, that you can build over time.

Invest within a clear and well-defined risk budget.

Uncertainty in many risk factors can be managed, to some extent if they are known, by the choice, allocation, timing and management of investments. The list below is not exhaustive but covers the main risks that the Trustee faces and how they can be managed:

- **Inflation risk**: The Trustee invests in a diversified range of assets that are likely to grow in real terms.

- **Pension conversion risk**: Proportioning of assets that closely match how we expect scheme members to use their allocated funds in retirement.

- **Market risk**: Primarily through investing in a diversified range of assets.

- **Counterparty risk**: Assess and manage counterparty risk through a rigorous approach to the procurement of a variety of investment services, regular monitoring, regular reports of the funds' underlying holdings and the fund manager's approach to managing risk.

- **Operational risk**: The Trustee, with its suppliers, assesses and manages its operational risks.

- **Liquidity/cash flow risk**: The Trustee invests in a diversified portfolio of assets that include liquid assets that can be quickly realised, as required. Cashflow forecasting is an important control and management tool to use.

- **Valuation risk**: Understanding the volatility of any asset class to ensure no default position occurs in funding or asset valuation thresholds, such as loan to value or leverage.

- **Environmental and social risks**: These risk factors can have a significant effect on the long-term performance of the assets held.

- **Governance risk**: This could be the manner in which we operate and comply with the defined rules externally to, or internally, within the SSAS.

- **Reputational risk**: The Trustee carefully selects its counterparties, manages its investments responsibly and considers all aspects of its reputation as part of its investment strategy.

Day-to-day operations

Typically, the Trustees may elect to appoint an external party to manage their assets to optimise return of time employed and access the correct level of resource expertise available.

Examples may include:

- Commercial property – commercial property agent

- Stocks and shares – stockbroker

- Managed funds – Fund manager

Responsible investment

In one of my books, 'Commercial to Residential Conversions: the essential manual for property developers', I cover the subject of responsible investment in detail and the following extract may be helpful in enabling you to assess what investment principles are correct for you, as you establish and remain true to your moral and ethical compass bearing.

The forward-thinking funders are beginning to take an increased interest in this area and in the future, I expect environmental sustainability to sit within the evaluation and due diligence criteria of funders and investors.

There are many interesting initiatives and processes that are emerging that are lead indicators as to where the world or business may be going, including:

- *Carbon cost accounting*

- *Natural capital accounting*

- *Green bonds*

- *Social impact bonds – remember our section earlier on how society is moving from an input based to an output-based economy.*

Environmental, Social and Governance (ESG) is a set of standards and criteria that increasingly socially conscious investors use for due diligence and screening of their investments. It considers how a company/investment opportunity stands scrutiny in each of the three areas.

1. *Environmental criteria consider the stewardship of the natural environment.*

2. *Social criteria scrutinise how it manages relationships with customers, employees, suppliers and the communities where it operates.*

3. *Governance observes how the company operates from shareholder structure and rights, leadership, internal controls and audit.*

When you have organisations like the European Investment Bank (EIB) and United Nations (UN) adopting this approach there will inevitably be much attention from the funding markets and sovereign wealth funds which will filter down to partial adoption and beyond, in the years to come.

Much work remains to be done in this area. However, I hope this has given you food for thought and the context, opportunity, accountability and responsibility that we as developers automatically assume when we take on our deeply meaningful societal role. Whether, and to what extent, we choose to adopt environmental sustainability could well have a fundamental effect on our economic sustainability in the future and the valuation on our business.

Communication, reporting and transparency

As Trustees you will have statutory levels of compliance to undertake. However, your Trust is a legal entity in its own right so treat its management information in a similar way to ensure you have the correct information available to enable decisions to be made at the right time, to take advantage of opportunity and address risk.

Types of communication of reporting may vary due to the size of SSAS or number of Trustees. However, it may typically include the following on a monthly, quarterly, bi-annually or annual basis:

• Balance Sheet

• Cashflow

• Risk register

• Committed cost schedule

• Budget

• Compliance schedule

Compliance with this SoIP

The Investment committee, that is established under this SoIP, is responsible for reviewing each of the elements and ensuring that all parties are aware of progress and that any delegated decision making is undertaken compliantly and with the required level of due diligence.

Appendix

Attach any useful criteria, structures, flow chart, targets or decision-making trees to enable simplicity and clarity to be available to all, and a clear record where progress can be monitored over time.

Which asset class?

One of the most crucial and also interesting decisions you will probably make within your SSAS is agreeing what asset classes to invest in. Due care and attention should be taken in selecting classes based on your experience, your time available, the risk profile, returns you expect and also your interest in the asset. Given that these assets may well be held for many years, it might be helpful to be interested in the subject matter at hand, although not entirely necessary.

Decide on the time that is available to you and your fellow Trustees and the expertise that is available to you. Many Trustees I know have decided that they wish to invest in asset classes that create cashflow and capital growth over lengthy periods of time and that require very little input of their time.

Considering your position, what decisions will you arrive at in defining what constitutes an attractive asset to your Trust. You may like to ask yourself the following questions:

- Has it got longevity?
- Is it secure?
- Does it create cashflow while you sleep?

- Is it compliant?
- Is it likely to grow in capital value?
- Can I force appreciation into the asset?

Given some of the questions above, it is very appealing within our SSAS to invest long-term in commercial property which enables us to benefit from all of the above considerations.

However, there are many types of asset classes for you to consider and whilst the very granular breakdown of compliant assets for a SSAS are contained in another chapter, the main classes are listed below:

- Property
- Intellectual property – such as my books
- Pension
- Stocks and shares
- Businesses
- Commodities
- Cash

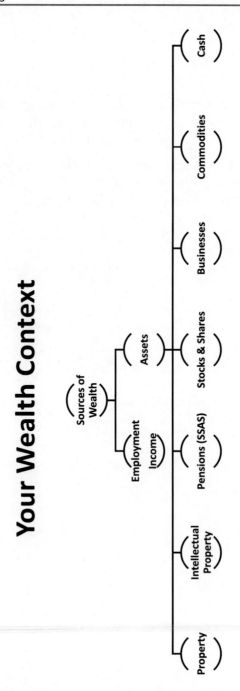

16. ACCELERATED COMPOUNDING

"Rule No. 1: Never lose money
Rule No. 2: Never forget rule No.1"

Warren Buffett

A SSAS is in no way a short-term strategy. It is not a get rich quick strategy and it inherently comes with a deep sense of accountability.

It is a long term, deeply personal and highly engaging strategy that is designed for the benefit of its members and will be best operated on with a long-term strategy and focus. This marries perfectly with the beauty of compounding.

Albert Einstein provides us with some fairly strong advice when he said that:

"Compound interest is the 8th wonder of the world. He who understands it, earns it; he who doesn't, pays it. Compound interest is the most powerful force in the universe".

The key is the power of compounding, the snowball effect that happens when your earnings generate even more earnings. You receive interest not only on your original investments, but also on any interest, dividends and capital gains that accumulate - so your money can grow faster and faster as the years roll on.

The Wonder of Compound Interest

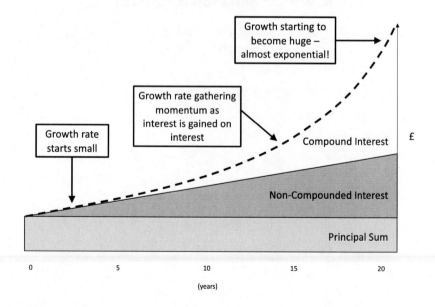

Compound interest can be defined as interest calculated on the initial principal and also on the accumulated interest of previous periods. Think of it as the cycle of earning 'interest on interest' which can cause wealth to rapidly snowball over time. Compound Interest will make a deposit or loan grow at a faster rate than simple interest, which is interest calculated only on the principal amount.

Not only are you getting interest on your initial investment, but you are getting interest on top of interest! It's because of this that your wealth can grow exponentially through compound interest, and why the idea of compounding returns is like putting your money to work for you.

Given the choice, would you rather have £500,000 up front, or 1 pence doubled every day for 30 days?

Most people would instinctively take the £500,000 but compound interest does not work on instinct - but maths.

Doubling up the initial 1 pence day one:

- It would be at day eight before you had more than £1

- After three weeks, however, you would have almost £10,500

- At day 30, your 1p would have become £5,368,709.12

Compounding is extremely powerful especially if you can harness it over time, and you should do all you can to ensure you maximise its force to your advantage.

That means realising that the earlier you invest and the more you have to invest will maximise the benefits of compounding. Then, as the pot builds, you will want it to remain as intact as possible, which means ideally avoiding income withdrawals and, particularly, any capital losses.

Preserve Capital: do not make losses and preserve your capital and interest earned. Any losses will set your compounding back significantly and momentum may be lost. This is important to understand when considering your risk/reward strategy of your SSAS in context with your age and therefore your reason for having a SSAS and retirement options.

Start Early: Compound interest favours those that start early, which is why it pays to start now. It's never too late to start — or too early. And that is why procrastination is a highly costly strategy in its own right. The earlier you start with a carefully thought out initial plan, the sooner the funds will start working for you. This is not specific to pensions but any long-term wealth growth plan.

Importance of Interest Rate: How significant is a 1% change in the interest rate to how much you earn with compound interest?

For a £1,000 initial investment at 4% interest, you would have £2,222 after 20 years and £4,801 after 40 years.

A 5% interest rate would give you £2,712 after 20 years and £7,040 after 40 years.

So, the very clear answer to the question is VERY significant! The three main components will always be capital sum, interest rate and time.

One very crucial consideration is how often the interest is compounded; an investment with interest compounded monthly will grow faster than an investment with interest compounded annually. While compound interest is beneficial if you are the one receiving the interest, if you are the one paying compound interest on a loan or credit card, then it's costing you a lot of money, as interest is charged on interest.

This might sound unrelated to SSAS, however, remember that you personally will be considering numerous angles whilst wearing different hats. You may be the SSAS Trustee, a Director of the sponsoring company, a parent looking at your legacy etc. Where does compounding fit into each vein of your overall wealth strategy?

The array of investment options available to SSAS Trustees makes compound interest even more lucrative given some of these key advantages:

1. A SSAS can leverage up to 50% of its fund value and invest that, increasing the compounding

2. The SSAS can invest in commercial property which can add very

significant 'leaps' to the fund valuation through:

a.   Planning gains after selling 'change of use' planning permissions on property or title splitting parts of a property.

b.   Revaluation of a property after rebasing commercial leases i.e. enhancing the terms thus increasing their value.

c.   Changing commercial leases to counter parties with a greater covenant strength, hence increasing the yield-based valuation.

2. The enablement of other opportunities outside of your SSAS, such as the benefit of selling a planning gain suggested in number one above and then developing it in another company, making a profit and then retaining the residential assets to growth in capital value over the coming decades whilst also generating positive cashflow on a monthly basis.

3. Reinvestment strategies of earned interest using a combination of all the points above

4. The SSAS is a highly tax efficient environment which significantly increases the additional accelerated compounding over time.

Now this is where the value creation really starts getting impressive.

Wow!! That is one compelling life wealth strategy in its purest form. And it can be something you can achieve with the right knowledge, counsel, support and resources.

And another thing - yes it keeps on getting better!

You are not doing this at the expense of others - you will actually be creating shared value for others along the way also. Now, how different is that to many corporate roles? Being able to create huge compounding personal wealth for you and your family as well as delivering value and growth to others at the same time. Truly a win:win.

This is the amazing **CREATING EXTRAORDINARY LEVELS OF COMPOUNDING WEALTH** that is the true power of a SSAS taking centre stage right at the very heart of a hugely compelling multi-generational wealth creation juggernaut!

Accelerated Compounding... it just gets better

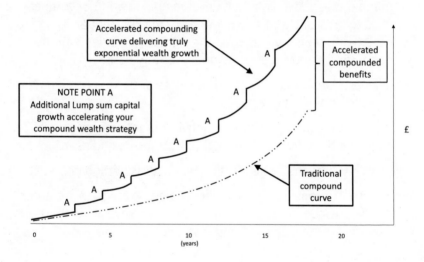

What are you waiting for? SSAS is waiting for you to explore it, the government and HMRC are encouraging you to understand it – IF it is right for you. SSAS Alliance is ready to help you on your journey and the benefits are there for you to taste, absorb and get excited about.

When you have this knowledge you truly start to understand that pensions are actually really exciting now!

17. TAX EFFICIENCY & PLANNING

"We contend that for a nation to try to tax itself into prosperity is like a man standing in a bucket and trying to lift himself up by the handle"

Winston S. Churchill

One of the principal attractions of SSAS pensions are their highly tax efficient array of benefits.

Any contributions that members make to a SSAS pension are eligible for tax relief. Basic rate taxpayers get a 25% tax top up, meaning HMRC adds £25 for every £100 you pay into your pension.

If you pay a higher rate of tax, you will be able to reclaim additional tax relief through your tax return. Contributions paid into the scheme by the employer also qualify for tax relief which can help reduce its total tax liability.

If you are a member of a SSAS pension you can start drawing benefits from the age of 55. Like all personal or workplace pensions you can choose to take the first 25% of your pension pot, as a tax-free lump sum, or receive 25% of each withdrawal tax-free.

The amount of benefits you are entitled to will depend on how much you and your employer has contributed to the scheme, how long each contribution has been invested and the performance of the investments.

After the tax-free amount, withdrawals will be subject to your normal rate of income tax. You can choose to take your pension as an income either by purchasing an annuity, or via income drawdown.

If you have individual existing pensions, you can transfer these into a SSAS. Before you make any decisions, though, it is important to get financial advice to ensure you don't lose any entitlements. You also need to be able to make an informed decision over whether the benefits of the transfer outweigh any downsides.

You can keep paying in until you reach a Government-directed maximum life-time allowance amount, after which you will lose some of the tax advantages. This amount is currently at £1,030,000 at the time of writing.

As the sponsoring employer, contributions you make to the pension will receive corporation tax relief. Personal contributions may also be made, and you could receive tax relief via your annual self-assessment tax submission process.

This initial tax relief is the key difference between a SSAS and other tax-friendly savings. As your pension grows, the fund is largely free of tax, aiding substantial compounding over time and all the while you have control over the money you are investing. It is this freedom of choice and control that draw many towards a SSAS pension.

Annual Allowance

The annual allowance is a limit on the total amount of contributions that can be paid to defined contribution pension schemes and the total amount of benefits that you can build up in defined benefit pension schemes each year, for tax relief purposes. The annual allowance is currently capped at £40,000 although a lower limit of £4,000 may apply if you have already started drawing a pension. The annual allowance applies across all of the schemes you belong to, it's not a 'per scheme' limit and includes all of the contributions that you or your employer pay, or anyone else who pays on your behalf.

If you exceed the annual allowance in a year, you will not receive tax relief on any contributions you pay that exceed the limit and you will be faced with an annual allowance charge.

The annual allowance charge will be added to the rest of your taxable income for the tax year in question, when determining your tax liability. Alternatively, if the annual allowance charge is more than £2,000, you can ask your pension scheme to pay the charge from your benefits. This means your pension scheme benefits would be reduced.

Unless you have a money purchase annual allowance (MPAA), you may be able to bring forward any unused annual allowances from the previous three tax years, to either reduce your annual allowance charge to a lower amount or reduce the annual allowance charge completely.

Be aware that any pension savings above the Lifetime Allowance are subject to the Lifetime Allowance charge. This charge will continue to be:

- 55% if the excess is taken as a lump sum

- 25% if the excess is taken as income, for example as a scheme pension, an annuity or drawdown. Income tax at your marginal rate will also be payable.

A simple calculation of £40,000 contributions per annum does not actually provide us with the full picture and you must discuss this with your accountant or financial advisor. For instance, HMRC are very clear that the £40,000 annual allowance is also linked to your earnings that year which effectively means that it is up to £40,000 capped at the limit of your salaried earnings. If you were on a salary of £28,000 then this would be your personal cap on contributions.

However, this does not apply when the employer is making the contribution. In this case, the earnings test is not applied and the maximum of £40,000 can be paid by the company, regardless of the earnings of the individual.

As an example, let us consider a SSAS which has 5 Trustees who have no other pension interests elsewhere. Their Lifetime Allowance per Trustee is £1,030,000, hence the SSAS Trust maximum valuation would be (preserving tax efficiency):

5 x £1,030,000 = £5,150,000

Careful tax planning and forecasting is required to ensure the tax efficiency that you have worked hard to achieve is not lost by breaching these thresholds through naivety or forethought.

For many, the very thought of achieving this level of growth in their SSAS is considered a nice problem to have, a 'first world problem' if you like. However, this is your hard-earned wealth which can continue to be a force for good in the world and I would strongly suggest that careful consideration and planning is a core skill in your SSAS toolkit, to preserve your wealth for both now, your retirement and possibly for future generations.

Lifetime allowance

The Lifetime Allowance is a limit on the amount of pension benefit that each individual can draw from pension schemes and can be paid without triggering an extra tax charge, including lump sums or retirement income.

Since April 2018, the Lifetime Allowance is £1,030,000 and it is likely to increase in line with Consumer Price Index inflationary levels at the end of each tax year. This is something to keep an eye out for each year in the Chancellor of the Exchequer's Budget speech!

The likelihood of you reaching your Lifetime Allowance will depend on a number of factors including:

- Level of contributions into pension to date
- Level of contributions into the pension in the future
- Growth rate of pension fund
- Investment strategy
- Duration of pension

While many people may initially feel they are not affected by the Lifetime Allowance, you should take action if the value of your pension benefits is approaching or likely to approach this limit. If you are younger, you never know how successful your strategies may be in the coming decades!

As pensions are normally a long-term commitment, what might appear a relatively small amount today could exceed the Lifetime Allowance by the time you want to take your benefits – particularly if you have taken the decision to have a SSAS and have operated it wisely and successfully!

It may be necessary to take your pension early or stop contributing to the scheme/plan, even though you have not retired, to avoid your benefits exceeding the Lifetime Allowance. The test for the Lifetime Allowance is done each time you access a pension benefit.

The Lifetime Allowance was introduced in 2006 and in subsequent years when it has been reduced. Following pension reforms, those with benefits valued in excess of the Lifetime Allowance have been able to apply for 'protection' to protect the value of benefits they have built up (and future benefits that may accrue) from tax charges.

These protections include:

- Primary protection
- Enhanced protection
- Fixed protection
- Individual protection

Each have different conditions attached to them.

An interesting question arises for Trustees who are part of the same Family SSAS when considering Lifetime Allowances.

Can the growth of your investments within your SSAS be allocated disproportionately to enable Lifetime Allowances to be met simultaneously?

Example: a married couple who have differing pensions pots within the same SSAS.

Angela has £350,00 and Neil has £80,000 in their pensions. Would their investment strategies over many years enable a dis-proportional allocation of growth to enable both Angela and Neil to arrive at the current Lifetime Allowance of £1,030,000, simultaneously?

This is something you should consider as part of your tax efficiency strategy - seek advice and counsel from your SSAS administrator and tax advisor to ensure you understand, and are aware of, all of the options available - and to ensure that above all, compliance is maintained.

A great source of information is the Pension Advisory Service Spotlights article https://www.pensionsadvisoryservice.org.uk/content/spotlights-files/uploads/Lifetime_Allowance_SPOT021_V3.0.pdf

In this article it refers to the method by which benefits are measured and when to comply with the Lifetime Allowance. The following is a useful extract:

"There is no limit on the amount of pension savings you can build up. However, there is a restriction on the amount of pension savings which a person may build up in a tax-favoured environment, and there is a tax charge if the total value of your pensions is more than this Lifetime Allowance. It is set at a high level, so it does not affect most people.

Whenever benefits are taken from a pension, you use up a percentage of the Lifetime Allowance. This is known as a Benefit Crystallisation Event (BCE). A BCE arises in the following circumstances:

- *Entering drawdown BCE1*
- *Entering scheme pension BCE2*
- *Scheme pension in payment increasing beyond a permitted margin BCE3*
- *Buying a lifetime annuity BCE4*
- *Reaching age 75 before taking all benefits from a defined benefit pension BCE5*
- *Reaching age 75 with a drawdown fund BCE5A*
- *Reaching age 75 before taking all benefits from a defined contribution pension BCE5B*
- *Funds on death under age 75 being used to provide draw down for dependant/nominee BCE5C*
- *Funds on death under age 75 being used to buy an annuity for dependant/nominee BCE5D*
- *Taking pension commencement lump sum (tax-free cash) BCE6*
- *Fund on death under age 75 being paid as a lump sum (BCE7)*
- *Transferring to a Recognised Overseas Pension Scheme (ROPS) (BCE8)*

- *Various one-off payments as prescribed in regulations (BCE9)*
- *The value of a BCE is normally the amount paid out or moved to provide retirement income. For defined benefit pensions, the value is normally treated as 20 times the initial amount of pension you receive plus any tax-free cash."*

Capital Allowances – BONUS SECTION

Many listening or reading to this book may be fellow property developers and may have read another of my books 'Commercial to Residential Conversions: The essential manual for property developers'.

One of the very significant advantages that many developers and commercial property investors value are capital allowances.

At this stage I want to be very clear with you that capital allowances are NOT directly applicable to a SSAS, which is already a tax efficient vehicle.

The clue though is in the word 'directly'. We have discussed earlier my passion for creating multiple compounding benefits through the use of a SSAS. Whilst not directly benefitting to the SSAS, a detailed awareness of capital allowances in all their forms are a great example of where additional and extremely valuable tax efficiencies can be deployed, within the overall sphere of your personal economy.

As an additional bonus, you will find the remainder of this section an exert from my book which I hope will be of particular interest in illuminating the compounded benefits you can access outside of the SSAS, from strategic considerations deployed in concert with the SSAS.

Capital allowances are a tax relief in lieu of depreciation and are claimed on the cost of plant and machinery existing within a commercial property.

They can significantly reduce tax liability, can sometimes result in a tax rebate and are therefore an important consideration in any property developers' tax planning. Specialist advice from a tax specialist(s) is again crucial in this area and interpreting the tax rules is essential.

It is possible to get tax relief on plant and machinery which can be defined broadly as:

- Heating
- Lighting
- Power Supplies
- Sanitary Ware and kitchen installations
- Carpeting
- Air conditioning

You cannot get tax relief on the following categories of a building:

- Foundations
- Bricks and Walls
- Roof
- Flooring
- Drainage

The summary components of a capital allowances tax relief claim include:

- Capital allowances can only be claimed once in the lifetime of any property – establish if there has been a historical claim.
- Allowances can be off set against any income stream.
- Sideways Loss Relief depending on the structuring of your group of companies.
- Holiday lets, serviced accommodation, commercial properties and certain residential works.
- Residential property generally is not allowable.
- From 5% - 150% of your capital investment can qualify.
- Can include purchase price of property and certain refurbishment costs.

- HMRC say 96% of available allowances have NOT been claimed!

It is important for the developer to agree the plant value in the building, with the vendor, within two years of purchase:

- Fail and you get nothing.

- Endeavour to agree as part of the sale negotiations.

- If the vendor will not agree – potential for a Tax Tribunal.

- It is a business cost in your accounts, reduces your 'taxable' profit and hence your tax.

- Only the 'owner' of the property can claim.

- Parties that may claim include:

  o   You

  o   Your spouse

  o   Partnership

  o   Limited company you control

- Non-Dwelling premises only.

A word of caution for you in this area. Whilst capital allowances can indeed be an incredibly powerful stimulus for your business as it is intended to be by HMRC, it is also an area where you will require specialist advice. You will require your accountant, a specialist capital allowances surveyor and possibly your solicitor to work closely together.

It is worth noting that you can outsource for advice, but you cannot outsource decision making and the ultimate accountability that comes with that. I strongly suggest that you use your accountant, solicitor and capital allowances surveyor to test each other's' opinions and advice to the point where maximum clarity is achieved before deploying this strategy. Failure to comply, or inaccurate use of the rules, will result in you and your business feeling the full weight of HMRC and their penalty process.

The legal entity that you are claiming capital allowances within can make a substantial difference in the tax efficiency of your strategy.

Certain legal entities are already highly tax efficient and therefore are unable to claim capital allowances. Two examples of this may include:

- Trusts
- Local Authorities/Government

Should your strategy and business be seeking the substantial benefits of capital allowances, you can certainly apply this knowledge when approaching and acquiring land, and commercial property opportunities, by understanding what legal entity the property is currently owned in which potentially could result in the most commercially beneficial advantage for you. A cautionary note would be to consider the lifetime of the ownership of the assets as previous owners could have claimed capital allowances and they can only be claimed ONCE.

Experience has generally shown that if your strategy is 'Buy, Develop, Sell' then the C3 use class apartments that you are creating would be held as 'stock' on the balance sheet in your SPV accounts, for a relatively short period of time and therefore would not be eligible under HMRC rules for capital allowances.

Should your strategy be 'Buy, Develop, Hold' then the apartments would be held as fixed assets on the balance sheet of your company and therefore capital allowances may well be something you should consider.

Once again, we see that the phrase 'start with the end in mind' will pay enormous dividends by ensuring you establish the correct structure and approach to your business interests. In identifying the type of property you are searching for and your intended purpose for that property, you will be able to incorporate the most appropriate advice from your professional team and ensure maximum efficiency and compliance over the term of your business interests.

There are numerous tax efficient allowances which you might consider with your specialist tax team, some of these include:

1. Capital Allowances: as discussed earlier in the chapter.

2. Enhanced Capital Allowances: The Enhanced Capital Allowance (ECA) energy scheme aims to encourage businesses to invest in certain energy saving technologies. The ECA energy scheme lets your business claim 100% first year tax relief on investments in qualifying technologies and products. This means you can write off (i.e. deduct) the whole cost, or up to the published claim value of buying the energy-saving product against your taxable profits in the year of purchase. ECA's bring forward tax relief so that you can set it against profits from a period earlier than would otherwise be the case.

3. Land Remediation Relief: Land Remediation Relief is a relief from corporation tax only. It provides a deduction of 100% plus an additional deduction of 50%, for qualifying expenditure incurred by companies in cleaning up land acquired from a third party in a contaminated state. Land Remediation Relief can enable up to 150% tax relief under certain circumstances - it pays to be informed! Land or buildings are in a contaminated state if there is contamination present as a result of industrial activity such that:

   - It is causing relevant harm.

   - There is a serious possibility that it could cause relevant harm.

   - It is causing, or there is a serious possibility that it could cause, significant pollution in the groundwater, streams, rivers or coastal waters.

'Relevant harm' includes significant adverse impact on the health of humans, animals or damage to buildings that has a real impact on the way the building is used.

Qualifying expenditure includes the cost of establishing the level of contamination, removing the contamination or containing it so that the possibility of relevant harm is removed. There is, however, no relief if the remediation work is not carried out.

Land Remediation Relief is available for both capital and revenue expenditure. However, the company must elect, within two years of the end of the accounting period in which the expenditure is incurred, to treat qualifying capital expenditure as a deduction in computing taxable profits.

In addition to the deduction for the cost of the land remediation, the company can claim an additional deduction in computing its taxable profits. This additional deduction is 50% of the qualifying expenditure. A company can claim this additional deduction at any time within the general time limit for claims under Corporation Tax Self-Assessment. HMRC does not specify any particular form for the claim. A computation reflecting the claim and submitted in time is sufficient. The 50% additional relief is given in the same period as the actual expenditure is charged to the profit and loss account.

I hope you enjoyed that exert from my other book and it has helped trigger some thoughts on how this specialist knowledge may be able to assist your wider economic interests in property. For instance, if you are investing in a commercial property in one of your other legal entities, using funds from a loan back as an example, then the knowledge of the power of capital allowances may well save you a very substantial amount of tax in the future.

Lateral thinking is extremely powerful. Your SSAS is NOT an isolated asset, it is one of possibly many parts of your personal wealth economy and there is no reason why you cannot look at how they interact with each other and serve your wider objectives - as long as each legal entity, including your SSAS Trust, acts with the correct governance, compliance and probity within each legal entity.

18. SETTING UP A SSAS

"Setting goals is the first step in turning the invisible into the visible"

Tony Robbins

The process of setting up a SSAS is not a particularly complicated process and with the support, guidance and advice of a small team of professionals you could move relatively quickly from initial discussions to SSAS establishment if you felt it was right for you.

Not everyone can establish a SSAS as we have discussed. There are strict HMRC qualifying criteria for those considering this route and an appropriately experienced Independent Financial Advisor, as well as a SSAS practitioner will be able to provide the correct advice, based on your particular circumstances.

The criteria for establishing a SSAS include:

- A SSAS is for business owners, directors and family members.

- The SSAS must be approved and registered with HMRC.

- Must have a scheme administrator.

- Must have a sponsoring company that has a trading history. You cannot just set up an 'off the shelf company'.

- The proposed sponsoring company must not be dormant.

- Requirement for scheme documentation including Trust Deed and Trust Rules.

- Requires a bank account.

- Registration of the scheme with The Pensions Regulator.

- Registration of the scheme with the Information Commissioner's Office responsible for promoting and enforcing the Data Protection Act 2018 and GDPR.

Timescales

Timescales to set up a SSAS can vary depending on personal circumstances. However, a timeline might look like this:

ACTION	TIMESCALE
Your investigation, gaining advice decision making and appointing your SSAS scheme administrator	Possibly 1-3 months however we all work at different tempos!
Scheme administrator prepares documentation for HMRC	2-4 weeks
HMRC approval and registration	2-4 months
Compliance, documentation, bank account etc	1-2 weeks
Transfer of funds from existing pension to new SSAS	1-3 months
TOTAL TIME (excluding decision making)	**Typically 4-7 months**

When our scheme was submitted to HMRC it was held up in a spot audit for 6 months with very little information or update available during this time for us to assess progress or any clarifications required. This can occasionally happen, however the process is now much slicker and can be done on line, reducing timescales. It was immensely frustrating! However, we used this time wisely, in research and planning, and finally once approved we were even better equipped to operate our SSAS.

On the other hand, I recently had a meeting with a great friend who runs a wealth building business and they have just experienced a three-week turnaround by HMRC of a SSAS which is a dramatic departure from the norm - in a good way!

Once the SSAS scheme is established and registered, your scheme administrator will oversee the processes of applying to the provider(s) of your existing pensions which you wish to transfer across. As noted before, you do not have to transfer all your pensions across choosing to leave some where they are. Your Independent Financial Advisor will be able to support you in deciding what is best for you.

One of my all-time best bits of advice I was ever given was to "walk a mile in another person's shoes" and this has served me well in several decades of extremely large international business and operational negotiations.

Think for a moment about the duty of care placed on your existing pension provider to ensure that they transfer the funds to a bona fide approved SSAS scheme. The government are placing very substantial obligations on financial institutions such as banks, pension providers and lenders to ensure they operate extensive Anti-Money Laundering (AML) checks. Whilst timescales may be longer than we expect and the level of apparent urgency is not demonstrated by everyone, let us take a certain degree of comfort that funds transfer are now much more closely scrutinised than they have been in the past, which must be seen as a positive step. Your SSAS will serve you and future generations very well in the coming decades; that is the 'size of the prize' to focus on and I hope it will provide some helpful context, if the initial set up period experiences a few weeks delay.

Costs

A very common question that I am asked is what the cost of running a SSAS is? The simple answer is not surprisingly, it depends!!

Some of the dependencies which will determine the cost base are as follows:

- How many Trustees in your SSAS?
- What your strategy is?
- How active your Trust is?
- Whether you choose to take on the responsibility yourself (not advised until you are very experienced, if ever)
- Professionalism of administrator

- The flexibility given by your SSAS administrator and the flexibility you require.

Let us take for example two SSAS Trusts:

Trust A: This Trust has 7 Trustees with a fund value of £1,200,000 and their strategy is:

- To acquire multiple commercial properties which require VAT registration.
- They have a loan back to two of their sponsoring companies.
- They have typically 2-3 loans at any time, with a 9-15 month duration each.
- Small amounts are invested through stocks and shares on a frequent basis.

Compare this very active strategy to Trust B.

Trust B: This Trust is a husband and wife with funds of £200,000. Their strategy is:

- 5 year loan back to their sponsoring company.
- Sale and lease back of their business premises.

As we can see, this illustrates very different levels of activity, administration, support, monitoring and reporting for those two Trusts and one would expect a different cost base.

In our various businesses we pay a fair market rate for great advice and do not shy away from it. In the past we have seen that low-cost advice, free help and 'opinion' has rarely been effective and quite often actually counter-productive. My suggestion is to do your research, establish a very credible team of advisors, negotiate hard but fair and pay them on time to ensure a very mutually rewarding relationship.

This reminds me of a quote I heard many years ago: "free advice is worth every penny"!!

Costs will vary between scheme administrators. We have seen fee structures vary from a fixed set up fee and then a fixed annual cost, irrespective of volume of activity through to a detailed fee schedule.

The important thing for you to be clear on is what is your strategy likely to be so that you are engaging on a basis that is right for you.

Fee structures from SSAS scheme administrators, as we have said, will vary substantially as will the level and detail of services they provide. The typical fee structures will probably be set out in 4 core areas:

1. SSAS Establishment

2. Administration

   a. Filings, notices and reporting compliance

   b. Setting up default bank account

   c. Contribution management

   d. Trustee management

3. Operational

   a. Meetings with Trustees

   b. Setting up an investment portfolio or platform

   c. Loans to sponsoring employer

   d. Property

   e. Property purchase

   f. Property sales

   g. Legal and searches

   h. VAT set up and administration

   i. Asset transfers

   j. In specie transfers

4. Benefit management

5. Ad hoc services – may be billed on an hourly rate so ensure you get a quote for ad hoc services.

Security of Trustee's funds

Each Trustee's share of the fund is held under Trust, is separate under law from the Trustee's personal wealth and the sponsoring employer's resources. However, Member Trustees must bear in mind that where SSAS funds are invested back into the sponsoring employer, for example by way of a loan or acquisition of its shares, or if the sponsoring employer is the tenant of a SSAS property and owes rent, the value of those assets may be reduced or lost if the sponsoring employer is placed into liquidation.

There is a risk warning over any form of investment, and you should consider this at length on EVERY investment. The value of investments may fall as well as rise, so you could get back less than you invest. It is therefore important that you understand the risks and commitments as well as a clear understanding of current legislation, taxation law and practice which may change from time to time - hence the need for great advisors.

SSAS bank account

Once notification has been received from HMRC that the scheme has been registered, a scheme bank account can then be opened up. Much tighter bank regulations are now in force and the bank will want to see verification of the SSAS, as they would with any legal entity prior to establishing a new and separate bank account for it.

Which bank account should you open up? Whilst technically it is entirely up to you and almost any bank will open a SSAS bank account for you. Practically though, unless you are planning to operate the SSAS and all its compliance yourself then generally, most Trustees will be operating by appointing a scheme administrator. They will open the bank account and undertake this process on your behalf, with you being sent bank account opening forms and mandates to complete and sign.

To aide their administration they will almost certainly have a favoured designated bank which they have a relationship with across their SSAS interests.

Your SSAS bank account is used to hold the SSAS's cash funds. All contributions and returns on investments must be paid into this account. The scheme administrator, as independent Trustee, may be the sole signatory to the account and will administer its day-to-day operation. However, the Trust Deeds and bank mandate will outline all the necessary governance agreed on how you structure your SSAS.

To equip you with a detailed overview of what you will be required to provide to establish a SSAS, I have included a list below. These items would be provided in the form of an application form or questionnaire from your scheme administrator well in advance for you to complete including.

- SSAS Name
- Number of Trustees
- Sponsoring employer details:
  o Company name
  o Contact details
  o Company status
  o Nature of business activities
  o Company registration number
  o Company year end
  o Company VAT number
  o Company Corporation Tax reference
  o Company PAYE reference
  o Number of employees
  o Address
  o Copy of Memorandum of Association
  o Copy of Article of Association

- Your Independent Financial Advisor (IFA):
  - o   Company name
  - o   Contact name
  - o   Address
  - o   Email
  - o   Who they are regulated by
  - o   Authorisation number
- Your investment advisor (if different to above)
  - o   Same details as IFA
- Trustees details:
  - o   Full name
  - o   Date of birth
  - o   Address
  - o   Email
  - o   Contact number
  - o   National Insurance Number
- Proposed Scheme Administrator
- Details of any investments into the SSAS
- Sponsoring employer declaration and signature
- Trustee declaration and signatures

The process to establishing your SSAS will proceed once the aforementioned information has been received. The scheme administrator, with you, will then proceed with the following:

- Submission and registration with HMRC
- Trust Deed
- Terms of business

- Sponsoring employer board minutes
- Resolution appointing advisers
- Data protection
- Bank mandate
- Compliance with HMRC and the Pension Regulator
- Transfer management

SSAS Scheme Rules

Every SSAS scheme requires a set of rules which reflect how the SSAS will be established, governed, controlled and prosper. Typical contents of the SSAS scheme rules might include:

1. Governance
2. Appointment and removal of Trustees
3. Investments
4. Power of Trustees
5. Help for Trustees
6. Proceedings of Trustees
7. Duties of Trustees
8. Liability of Trustees
9. Fees of Trustees
10. Costs of the SSAS
11. Scheme administrator
12. Employers
13. Admission of membership
14. Contributions
15. Multiple individual funds

16. Benefits for a member

17. Death Benefits

18. Drawdown

19. Payment of lump sum death benefits

20. Transfer of benefits

21. Payment of benefits

22. Overpayment of benefits

23. Deduction of tax

24. Application of general fund

25. Pension sharing

26. Buying out benefit

27. Winding up

28. Notices

29. Definitions and interpretation

19. CONTRIBUTIONS TO YOUR SSAS

**"When you cease to make
a contribution, you begin to die"**

Eleanor Roosevelt

A SSAS provides a lot of flexibility in how contributions are made. Sponsoring employers, Trustees and third parties can contribute to the SSAS with any third-party contributions being treated as Trustee contributions. Contributions allowed can be paid on a regular or one-off basis.

Employer contributions are paid gross and amounts are taken into account for the purposes of a Trustee's Annual Allowance. A sponsoring employer will only get full tax relief for its contributions, as a business expense, if HMRC accepts that the expense is incurred 'wholly and exclusively' for the purposes of the employer's trade or profession.

A sponsoring employer can only pay contributions for Trustees who are its employees. Each Trustee can request their employer for part of their employee earnings to be given up and paid to the SSAS as an employer contribution. This is known as 'salary sacrifice' and as always, financial advice should be taken.

The maximum Trustee contributions in any tax year are restricted to 100% of relevant UK earnings which are chargeable to Income Tax for that tax year.

The total gross amount of all contributions including those from a sponsoring employer, to the SSAS and any other registered pension schemes in that tax year, must not exceed the Trustee's available Annual Allowance, Money Purchase Annual Allowance or Tapered Annual Allowance.

Annual Allowance

The Annual Allowance is the upper limit in any tax year, on the total value of contributions paid by, or for a Trustee to the SSAS, and any other registered pension schemes they may have. This also includes any benefit increases in Defined Benefit schemes in that tax year that can benefit from tax relief.

The current level of Annual Allowance is £40,000 gross.

Money Purchase Annual Allowance

A Trustee can flexibly access benefits by taking an uncrystallised fund pension lump sum. Should they decide to do this, then the Money Purchase Annual Allowance will apply.

The Money Purchase Annual Allowance is the upper limit for a tax year, on the total value of contributions paid by, or for a Trustee to the SSAS, and any other money purchase registered pension schemes they may have, that can benefit from tax relief.

For the tax year 2018/19 the Money Purchase Annual Allowance is £4,000 gross.

Tapered Annual Allowance

Tapered Annual Allowance applies in a tax year if a Trustee's earnings, including any dividends, interest on savings and pension contributions exceed £150,000 in the tax year. This is known as the Adjusted Income.

Should these earnings exceed £150,000 then the Tapered Annual Allowance mechanism reduces the Trustee's Annual Allowance for that year on a sliding scale. For every £2 of adjusted income over £150,000, the Annual Allowance will be reduced by £1 down to a minimum of £10,000 gross.

The Annual allowance is currently £40,000 hence Adjusted Income would have to be at £210,000 for the Tapered Annual Allowance to draw the Annual Allowance down to its minimum level of £10,000.

The calculation for this is:

£210,000-£150,000 = £60,000

£60,000 reduced by £1 for every £2 exceeded = £30,000

Annual Allowance of £40,000 - £30,000 = £10,000

The Tapered Annual Allowance does not apply if a Trustee's 'threshold income' for the same tax year is £110,000 or less even if they have adjusted income of £150,000 or more.

Carry forward of unused allowances

A Trustee can carry forward any unused Annual Allowance or Tapered Annual Allowance to a tax year, from one or more of the immediately preceding three tax years provided the Trustee was a member of a registered pension scheme, in each relevant year, and is not subject to the Money Purchase Annual Allowance.

For example: Luke has had a pension for many years but since leaving his corporate employment to focus on his property business 4 years ago, has not continued to pay annual contributions.

It is now February and Luke is in a position where he can take advantage of his Annual Allowance, having substantial income.

Luke chooses to make three payments of £40,000 gross into his SSAS for the prior years based on carry forward, totalling £120,000. In addition, Luke will be able to make a further £40,000 contribution in the new tax year starting in April. A highly tax efficient position for Luke.

Luke is now considering how the additional total of £160,000 contribution into his SSAS will be invested in the months to come.

Transfers from other pension schemes

A SSAS can accept transfers for Trustees from other registered pension schemes which will be added to their share of the SSAS fund, enabling consolidation under the SSAS.

Trustees should seek professional financial advice as to the suitability of a transfer. In the case of a transfer from a defined benefit (final salary) registered pension scheme, they would usually be required to obtain and provide evidence of such suitable advice to the final salary defined benefit scheme provider. This would be undertaken by a suitably qualified Independent Financial Advisor.

It is extremely important that you listen and consider this advice, probing with educated questions. There are still some extremely generous defined benefit schemes on very favourable terms and whether you decide to remain with your current provider or establish a SSAS, will depend on many of the factors we have considered include the independent advice. Please carefully consider your ability to invest any funds through a SSAS to create a sustainable return that exceeds your risk adjusted return profile currently.

Transfers are not allowed from a defined benefit unfunded public sector scheme. Examples of these may include:

- NHS Scheme
- Armed Forces
- Teachers Scheme
- Civil Service Scheme
- Police
- Firefighters

There is no tax relief on a transfer from a registered pension scheme and they do not count towards the Annual Allowance.

To recap on a few key 'upsides' covered elsewhere in the book of potential advantages of transferring pensions into a SSAS:

- Consolidate pensions into a single scheme
- Reduce administration and costs
- Wide range of investment opportunities
- Control over the investment strategy and investments
- Wide range of retirement benefit options
- Flexible death benefits
- General Unallocated Fund

General Unallocated Fund

A General Unallocated Fund is unique to a SSAS and is available to Trusts which have a minimum of 2 members.

A SSAS can receive large pension contributions up to £500k and receive corporation tax relief in the current year by utilising a General Unallocated Fund within the SSAS scheme.

If a Business has made large profits and wishes to make a pension contribution for its directors, it can make a contribution of up to £500,000 which will be allocated to a General Unallocated Fund within the SSAS.

The Company would receive £100,000 corporation tax relief (assuming a 20% rate) in the current year. The SSAS will have £500,000 with which to make investments from the contribution date of the funds.

The General Unallocated Fund is then allocated to the Trustee's fund over time, in lieu of future contributions for Trustees within HMRC limits. This fund may be invested and borrowed from as with any other part of the fund.

This fund can take contributions either in cash or in-specie, from the sponsoring employer and that employer can receive tax relief on contributions up to a maximum of £500,000 per annum.

As we can see in the area of SSAS contributions, there are many ways to contribute to maintaining the high level of tax privilege afforded to the Trustees. However, ensuring that that privilege does not turn into a liability by breaching rules, is crucial in preserving capital and compliance. So, take great and regular advice from your SSAS Administrator, Independent Financial Advisor and tax advisor to ensure your governance and compliance remains immaculate!

20. OPERATING A SSAS

"There are no secrets to success. It is the result of preparation, hard work, and learning from failure"

Colin Powell

Once the SSAS has been established and registered with HMRC, funds can be paid into the Trustee's bank account by way of contributions from the sponsoring employer, from members and transfers from members other pension schemes.

The Trustees invest the funds prudently which is a requirement under Trust law, to try to achieve growth in interest, dividends, income and capital growth.

The value of each Trustees share in the SSAS fund will depend on the contributions and transfers paid in by, or for them, their share of any investment growth or loss, and any relevant payments made from the SSAS for them in the form of benefits.

If Trustees are to share in the overall performance of the investments in the SSAS fund, then each Trustee's share, at any time will be calculated as a percentage of the entire SSAS fund.

By prior agreement of the Trustees, shares can be directly linked to the performance of certain investments. This type of structuring would require the agreement of all Trustees and recorded in a documented Trustee resolution.

The amount of the benefits that a Trustee can receive will depend on the value of their share of the SSAS fund at the time they decide to take benefits.

It is the Trustee's responsibility to check the draft annual statement each year, prior to approval, to ensure that each Trustee's individual allocation of the fund is recorded accurately. Over time this can become quite complex and is something that you should work closely with your fellow Trustees and scheme administrator to ensure no conflict, disagreement or non-clarity occurs.

Compliance

A SSAS is set up under a Trust by the employer for the benefit of invited employees. As such, it is an occupational pension scheme, meaning the regulatory oversight falls on The Pensions Regulator.

Since 6 April 2006, there has been no requirement for a SSAS to have an independent pension Trustee to manage its administration. While some SSAS's have continued employing an independent administrator, others have elected to save costs and perform the duties themselves.

Given the significant penalties from HMRC for non-compliance, this is not an area to take risks or use 'soundbites' to manage your SSAS.

Unauthorised Payments & Penalties

Prior to 2006, if a SSAS had an error in its reporting or investments, rather than instantly raising a penalty or tax charge, Trustees were often given a 90-day period in which to correct the position or remove the offending investment from the scheme. If complied with, the scheme was permitted to continue without penalty.

Now, no such period of grace exists and under the current regime, once a breach has occurred, a tax penalty will be incurred. Even if the breach is corrected, with no advantage gained by any connected party or without any loss of revenue to the Treasury, the tax penalty will still be owed.

Depending on the breach, a tax penalty might fall on one or more of the founder employers, a scheme member or the scheme itself.

Breaches may also occur in providing the scheme's administrative functions. Failure to provide annual member statements – or Lifetime Allowance statements where benefits have come into payment – is a breach of duties, as is the non-deduction and accounting for tax due on any benefit payments.

Sadly, in several of these examples, there is nothing to be done but correct the issue and pay any tax or penalty due.

Fines can be issued by HMRC if there is no professional scheme administrator and formal duties of administering the scheme rest with members not carrying them out correctly.

Fines can vary from £100 plus £60 a day for failing to submit a pension scheme return, up to £3,000 for providing incorrect information/ submitting incorrect pension scheme returns and 14 years in jail for money laundering.

HMRC is not the only organisation to monitor SSAS's. They are also regulated by the Pensions Regulator, Information Commission and anti-money laundering regulations.

Penalty levels for compliance failures can be extensive and wide ranging and just some of the examples are shown below:

- The Pensions Regulator can impose fines of £50,000 where regulation breaches have occurred
- Data protection non-compliance can total £500,000
- Failure to provide information requested: £300 plus £60 a day
- Negligent or fraudulent provision of incorrect information: up to £3,000
- Failure to keep records or documents: up to £3,000
- Failure to submit a Pension Scheme Return: £100 plus £60 a day
- Negligent or fraudulent submission of an incorrect Pension Scheme Return: up to £3,000
- Failure to produce documents requested: £300 plus £60 a day
- Negligent or fraudulent production of incorrect documents: up to £3,000
- Failure to submit an accounting for tax form: £100 per quarter for each ten reportable individuals
- Negligent or fraudulent production of an incorrect Accounting for Tax Return: the unpaid tax due
- Serious breaches of regulations resulting in penalties imposed by HMRC Tribunal: 40% of the value of the fund, withdrawal of the pension scheme's registered status and the fund becomes fully taxable
- Unauthorised payment charges for non-allowable investments or incorrectly calculated benefits: tax charges of between 55% and 70% imposed on the recipient of the funds and the Scheme Administrator

The purchase of Taxable Property will be subject to the Unauthorised Payment Charge by HM Revenue & Customs.

The Unauthorised Payments Charge is a minimum of 55% of the value of the investment but the tax charge can exceed 70% and even cause the Scheme to be deregistered, which will have tax consequences on the entire SSAS.

The investment does not benefit from the usual tax advantages that apply to pension scheme investments - the income is taxable and any capital gains on disposal is also taxable. For these reasons it is very tax inefficient to hold Taxable Property in a SSAS.

Keeping The Pensions Regulator informed

The law requires that Trustees must provide certain information at certain times and in particular circumstances to The Pension Regulator (TPR).

The appointment of a scheme administrator is normally how most Trustees fulfil the majority of their obligations in this regard.

Trustees must supply TPR with information for their register of pension schemes and complete regular scheme returns. They will also have to inform when particular scheme or employer-related events and certain breaches of the law happen.

The information you have to provide to TPR includes:

• Providing information for the register and the scheme return. This return requests:

    o   the information needed for the register.

    o   other information TPR reasonably need to carry out their duties, for example, to assess the risks for each scheme.

Scheme returns can be completed on-line and come pre-filled with information that TPR already hold on the Trust. However, this should always be checked and is something your scheme administrator will do. The scheme return notice makes it clear the date by which the Trustees must complete and send the return back.

- Notifiable events - Notifiable events are designed to provide a warning system. Where a scheme is eligible to cover from the Pension Protection Fund (PPF) they alert TPR to a potential employer insolvency or to problems with the funding of the scheme. This allows the TPR time to try and help improve the situation before a claim on the PPF becomes inevitable. Notifiable events are scheme-related or employer-related. Trustees of schemes with a defined benefit element have to report to TPR when particular scheme-related events happen. Sponsoring employers of these schemes must notify when particular employer-related events happen.

An example of a scheme-related event is two or more changes to the post of scheme administrator within a 12 month period.

An example of an employer-related event is any decision by the employer in ceasing to carry on business in the UK.

- Breaches of the law - Trustees must report certain breaches of the law to TPR. This duty is often known as 'whistleblowing'. This places a duty on Trustees, employers, professional advisers and others to report when they reasonably believe that a legal duty relevant to the administration of the scheme has not, or is not being met, and that it is materially significant to TPR.

Governance

As with running any business entity, the principles of solid governance continue to apply in a SSAS Trust. You will have a clear set of rules and obligations to comply with for HMRC and The Pension Regulator.

The other consideration that should not be taken lightly is the responsibility that you have to your fellow Trustees.

If there is more than one Trustee you will need to keep additional records to ensure that all Trustees fully understand their responsibilities, have contributed and agree with the Statement of Investment Principles and regularly engage, contribute and understand the evolution of the SSAS.

Agree an annual diary of Trustee meetings in advance to ensure optimum attendance and keep detailed minutes of discussions and resolutions. It is also sensible to keep your scheme administrator involved with your SSAS strategy and progress and invite them to attend or dial in on a regular conference call can prove particularly beneficial as you build long term relationships.

21. KNOW YOUR FUND VALUATION

"A man must be big enough to admit his mistakes, smart enough to profit from them and strong enough to correct them"

John C. Maxwell

Given that to most people their pension is the largest 'bank account' they own, it is perhaps surprising that a very small percentage of the population actually know what the value of their pension is. We discussed earlier in the book about transfer values of current pension schemes or Cash Equivalent Transfer Value (CETV) as it is known.

The principle of understanding the valuation of your fund and the forecasting of it moving forward should never leave your subconscious thought. It is the fundamental to much of the mechanics that enable you to operate a SSAS to its optimum effect.

Once you have a SSAS there are five fundamental reasons why you should understand what your fund value is on a regular basis:

1. **Growth:** The growth rate of your Fund – presumably this is one of the core reasons you are operating your SSAS!

2. **Maintain:** To enable you to decide what, within your SSAS fund, is working effectively and what requires attention. You may find that certain assets or asset classes are underperforming and may require disposal or others working particularly well and requiring additional concentration and investment.

3. **Leverage:** Your SSAS fund can leverage (borrow) up to 50% of the fund value. You should monitor this level from a compliance perspective as well as from an opportunity angle.

4. **Loan Back:** You can loan up to 50% of the fund value to your sponsoring company(s).

5. **Compliance:** Given that punitive tax penalties exist for failure to comply with SSAS rules set out by HMRC, it is important for you to continually assess the above -particularly in relation to points 3 and 4.

Your SSAS may be structured with anywhere between one and eleven Trustees. Each Trustee has a proportion of the Trust fund valuation at any time. Each Trustee has a specific personal requirement for their proportion of that fund long term, which may include providing a pension in later life. It is important that the fund valuation is reported on a regular basis to ensure that this is understood and audited to the satisfaction of each Trustee.

The Trustees, normally via their Trust administrator, should ensure that there are financial statements prepared every year, setting out the fund valuation in total and the allocation of the total fund between the members.

The financial statements can take the form of a simple balance sheet, more formal accounts or even audited accounts, depending on the Trustees' requirements.

In between accounting periods for reasons quite often associated with a larger investment, the scheme administrator can commission an ad hoc or informal update at the direction of the Trustees.

22. BANK GRADE DUE DILIGENCE

**"Judge a person by their questions
rather than their answers"**

Voltaire

At the start of this critical chapter of the book I want to highlight TWO major points already raised in the book: These must be clearly understood, and I make no apologies for reinforcing these points regularly throughout the book.

- A SSAS Trust is a business and must be run as such.

- With a SSAS **YOU** become the bank! You must start acting like one.

Before you proceed any further with investigating a SSAS, look in the mirror and have a word with yourself please!

Once you have this mind-set very clearly established things will change very quickly for the better. You now have what others may want. You become valuable in even more ways than you were before. This is NOT just a wonderful feeling but is also something you must control and take responsibility for. It is your future, your wealth creation strategy and something you and your fellow Trustees must cherish, protect and define your own specific path.

As you are now a 'bank', a fundamental part of your process moving forward will include Bank Grade Due Diligence.

The one absolute certainty with a SSAS is that you must do something with your funds. If you do not, the funds will sit in the bank and rot – at the time of writing, bank base rates are at 0.75% which is circa 2% below the rate of inflation.

Compounding works on a positive AND negative basis. Imagine the damage to your precious capital if the funds were to sit there and rot year after year through ignorance, paralysis or procrastination.

You will now be starting to understand why we coined the phrase 'Bank Grade Due Diligence' – because you are the bank!

Like any business, whether a limited company, limited liability partnership, charity or Trust, each have an obligation to their stakeholders to run their organisation in a compliant and responsible manner - in the interests of the shareholders, or in our case, the Trustees.

Interestingly from one of my other businesses perspective which is actively engaged in large scale commercial property acquisition and redevelopment, there is an example which brings the point home in a different way.

A development organisation by its nature usually requires very substantial amounts of senior debt from a bank. The bank will have a comprehensive security package that you will be required to sign up to, and adhere to, including first legal charge on the property registered at land registry, a debenture on the special purpose vehicle development company and personal guarantees from the directors. This ensures that, without question, the bank are the first to be paid back from any funds resulting from the development and they are first in the queue for any remedial action, in the event of a default.

Despite this extremely comprehensive security package there is one party that can trump this security - that is HMRC.

When might this occur? Well if the development business (in this example) had not been operwated correctly with poor governance and had failed to pay its taxes, then HMRC may place a demand and pursue unpaid taxes.

How can the senior debt lending bank protect their interest as far as is reasonably practicable from this event? Well, they undertake due diligence on the directors beforehand to assure themselves that they are competent, have business track record, can evidence their experience, assess the calibre of their selected professional team and advisors and have the pedigree to deliver the development - and identify and manage any risks along the way.

Due diligence for your SSAS starts at home. It starts with the basic business housekeeping like any organisation. Create a systemised suite of processes that become your 'checklist'. This will include areas to consistently operate, evaluate, consider and utilise the best calibre and most appropriate proven external resources to support your organisation.

Like all good systems they evolve over time through constant use, learning and channelling of lessons encountered, into them and therefore becoming increasingly more comprehensive as time passes. Our bank grade due diligence Development Analyser, in our development business, is now in its 52nd revision at the time of writing and that will continue to increase as we channel all our learning into it, as externalities, circumstances and strategy change and evolve.

Your due diligence system will need to be similar. View it as the backbone of your Trust, evolving it through tweaks and revisions each time new learning, situations and approaches are experienced.

There will be many reasons for undertaking due diligence:

- Identifying and managing risk
- Demonstrating HMRC adherence
- Protecting your tax efficiency
- Avoiding penalties
- Ensuring you only invest in sound opportunities and screen out inappropriate options
- Optimising each investment
- Evaluating counter-party risk and reward
- To capture learning and create checklists
- Establishing an audit trail

The types of due diligence can be extensive and will depend on the nature and interests of the Trustees and their investment strategy. For instance, if the strategy was predominantly focused on share portfolios then due diligence might appear to be radically different to another SSAS for whom commercial property is their focus. However, there will be consistent factors across both businesses that maintain solid governance and controls. These types of due diligence might include:

- Sensitivity analysis
- Cashflow forecasting and Trust liquidity

- Reviews of your professional team

- Fellow Trustees' engagement and debate

- Appraisal of each investment opportunity

- The directors/partners/Trustees that are bringing you the opportunity for consideration

- Thorough understanding of all costs

- Analysis of returns

- Risk management

- Funding structure

- Compliance

- Fund valuation

When you undertake your due diligence, anything you fail to identify at this stage, which later emerges and impacts your decision-making process, could be extremely expensive. In terms of return on investment, proper structured investment at the start of your process, will ensure that your evaluation criteria are formed on solid bedrock, not on shifting sand.

We have invested heavily in creating a nationally renowned Development Analysis tool. We refer to our due diligence as bank grade due diligence and quite rightly so, given the fundamental reliance of any commercial conversion and development is on the utilisation of leverage from commercial funders. Therefore, our due diligence must stand the rigours and robust testing and evaluation of our funders, credit risk department and their policies.

If you would like to know more on how to be fully trained and access our Development Analysis Tool, then visit www.markstokesuk.com

"Walk a mile in another person's shoes" is one of the most valuable pieces of advice I was ever given over two decades ago and has stood me in very good stead ever since.

Bank grade due diligence is crucial to understanding how each one of our stakeholders will evaluate, whether that be our commercial funding partners, private investors, valuers, and many of the other areas we will look at later on in the process. Once you have systemised your due diligence it will become a relatively swift process to get the core data and initial assessment undertaken. You may be able to get your initial due diligence concluded within a matter of hours while initially, as you start your journey in evaluating developments, this may well take several days. However, with a systemised approach, you will be able to improve on this substantially.

SSAS schemes are designed to provide comprehensive, yet flexible investment opportunities from an extensive range of asset classes open for consideration. As Trustees, we will need to be mindful of HMRC rules - as we discuss at length in a separate chapter - where there are some investments that we will be unable to consider without falling foul of stringent penalties and losing our tax efficient status.

You may find that your SSAS administrator may require you to demonstrate to them that you have taken the appropriate due diligence from a suitably qualified and independent party in order for them to approve and transact the investment opportunity. A case in point would be using a solicitor and RICS valuation for the purchase of a commercial property or piece of land.

This should not be a surprising fact to anyone, but it usually is.

Bank Grade Due Diligence has a cost. In fact, Bank Grade Due diligence **MUST** cost money.

If you 'nickel and dime' the process and call in favours, you will end up with a mixed bag of unrelated opinions. My advice is always to engage the experts and do it in a structured way. What you are looking for is a risk assurance model that enables you to have recourse should later down the line issues arise. How do you think the banks recovered some of their catastrophic position post the financial crisis in 2009/2010?

They went to their contracts and challenged the professional indemnity insurance of their valuation surveyors and legal team.

Without contracts and by using favours, they would have yes, reduced their short-term cost base but secondly provided no accountability long term.

Why would you think of doing that? Remember, as a SSAS Trust, you are the bank.

"He who has the Peso's has the say so's!!"

Your voice counts! You can start to dictate the terms of your loans and investment decisions, or at least define investment criteria. They will need to be realistic. However, this will then give you a yard stick to gauge your due diligence against.

If proper due diligence has not been undertaken, the "truth will emerge after the costs have been spent".

Think of the time and costs you might spend on due diligence. This might be for a property purchase which could include legal and valuation fees, surveys etc which can run well into £10,000+ in some cases. Make sure your Bank Grade Due Diligence commences right from the initial analysis stage as your SSAS capital base will repeatedly take dents if you get this wrong, having spent the costs on fees and surveys etc, only for the deal to fall apart.

This can often happen for the unwary when there is a bank bringing leverage. If this is a commercial finance or a development loan and flaws appear in your due diligence, the bank may decide the deal is un-fundable and this could spell the end of your deal and the wasting of valuable 'seed cost' invested in the due diligence up front.

Be very wary of this but also become empowered by it. You have the reins, you need to understand how to take control and guide your decision making.

This is a liberating feeling and perfectly achievable once you are clear on your strategy.

Be your own Credit Committee

If you have ever had a commercial finance product, mortgage or development loan you may well be familiar with credit committees. These are bank committees who evaluate each commercial funding opportunity before signing off and approving the loan.

The credit committee would include members of senior management, compliance and technical departments and would call on pre-prepared information to appropriately consider submitted investments, on a weekly or fortnightly basis.

How would you like to turn the tables and become the credit committee?

Well with your SSAS you can and indeed SHOULD!

As we know, a SSAS can make loans to unconnected third parties. It would make business sense to establish clear criteria with your Trustees of who, how, when and on what basis you would make loans from your SSAS.

Initially you may be going out seeking funding/investment opportunities, however as you become more confident and meet more people you will become more immersed and renown and something remarkable will happen. You will become a magnet for opportunity. Opportunity will be drawn towards you for you to consider – and consider you must!

Would you make a loan to a land developer if you knew nothing about property development? Probably not unless there was something more compelling such as a security package that provided comfort, a clear exit strategy, the opportunity to earn and learn and you had independent advice that could be relied upon.

New SSAS Trustees will have come from a wide variety of backgrounds and hence their source of funds will have come from many different disciplines, employment positions etc. Some will have spent many years in scarcity mode, believing that they have no access to money, looking for money from private investors and saving hard - or not as the case may be. Others may have come from an abundance background of having adequate source of funds, family money to access and multiple areas to engage investment funds and leverage.

Bringing a SSAS into play now provides an entirely different set of options available to many.

For many it will be the largest bank account that they have ever had

Exciting? Absolutely!

Daunting? Quite probably!

Thought provoking? Definitely!

Imagine a time not too far away - you now have the funds available in your SSAS bank account. They are yours now to plan and invest with whom and how you see fit, all within the rules, of course, and with any fellow Trustees.

As a group of Trustees, it would be sensible to plan what your strategy is (see chapter on 'strategy' where we discuss Statement of Investment Principles) and understand your risk/reward appetite. Once you are very clear on this you can save yourself, and others, a great deal of time by sending the right signals out that you are open for business on this clear basis and can therefore attract the right type of opportunity matching your criteria.

Exciting times indeed for you and your fellow Trustees.

SSAS scams

Inevitably in our increasingly connected world, scams are unfortunately common place. They happen sadly in so many walks of life and can vary from preying on the vulnerable to extremely sophisticated. We have all probably had the email from the African Prince who has unearthed an inheritance and has specifically asked you for your help!! What could possibly go wrong?!

Given that SSAS Trustees have access to substantial sums of money by their nature, it is hardly surprising that there is an increasing focus on SSAS's being targeted by scammers trying to get their hands on any economic ill-gotten gain by preying on the uneducated and unwary.

There are several types of scam where the scammer convinces a potential investor to transfer funds from a legitimate scheme into what looks like a bona fide SSAS, which is however, a fraudulent one.

Firstly, a proportion of the newly invested funds are paid direct to the pension investor in the form of 'cash back' or a 'non-repayable loan'.

It is likely that HMRC could consider that either of these are unauthorised payments. If that is the case, then the individual could well be hit with significant tax charges.

The next possible stage could be the scammer suggests investing the remainder of the funds into a non-mainstream investment, but with the allure of high returns.

Nothing much then happens until, 12 months later, the investor tries to make contact for the annual review to see how the investment is performing. This proves impossible because the scammers have disappeared, along with the individual's pension funds.

Here are a number of things to look out for in spotting potential scammers:

How long has the receiving SSAS been established? Check by asking to see the Trust deed.

- Be aware of cold callers. They may be offering incredible opportunities and guaranteed returns and prey on the feeling of FOMO – Fear of Missing Out. Professional advisors, who are regulated, cannot and do not offer any form of guarantee on returns so be on high alert for any call or contact making these types of suggestions.

- Can you find any evidence of the company behind the SSAS? Search online to find evidence that the company behind the SSAS is 'bona fide' and actually trading. Check Companies House, websites, social media profiles etc to find any evidence of an operating footprint.

- Check the scheme administrator? If there is a company involved as the scheme administrator, but they are not a Trustee of the scheme, then be wary. If a SSAS administrator is formally engaged, then this could be a positive indicator that all is well – however, conduct all checks necessary.

Check your SSAS scheme administrator's policy which helps to protect their clients from some very real data security risks, including:

• Breaches of Confidentiality - For instance, information being given out inappropriately.

• Failing to offer choice - All individuals should be free to choose how the company uses data relating to them.

• Reputational damage - For instance, the SSAS could suffer if 'hackers' successfully gained access to sensitive data.

Last but by certainly not least on due diligence and something that is often overlooked, is the crucial importance of listening to your gut feeling.

In my previous career I used to be a corporate trouble shooter for over 20 years and have seen and experienced many situations - and you learn from each and every one in different ways. I know from when I have made mistakes over the years and then logically analysed where that came from - and how I could have improved - I can invariably trace back to an earlier time when something just simply didn't feel right, and I didn't heed the warning.

If there is a feeling in your water that something doesn't feel right, do not ignore it, follow it up and dig into it further. You will probably find the reason quite quickly and it could alter your decision to proceed, or how you proceed and save you time, cost and anxiety and worry in the future.

I do not think you can put a price on laying your head on the pillow at night and sleeping easy. Without that the world can rapidly feel like a tough place indeed. Let us be honest with each other – you probably didn't enter your chosen strategy, be that SSAS pensions or any business venture, by massively increasing stress on your life, so listen to your gut and it will generally serve you well.

23. WHAT YOU CAN DO WITH YOUR SSAS?

"Take advantage of every opportunity to practice your communication skills so that when important occasions arise, you will have the gift, the style, the sharpness, the clarity, and the emotions to affect other people"

Jim Rohn

The beauty of a SSAS pension that attracts many, is the diversity of investment opportunities that are available for those who seek ownership, choice and control of their decisions.

The following is a comprehesive list of the range of assets permitted by HMRC, at the time of writing, for a SSAS to invest in:

- Commercial Property

  Industrial property

  Retail Units

  Agricultural Land

  Commercial Land

  Industrial/business units and warehouses

  Offices and shops

  Forestry and woodland

  Land for development

  Public houses

  Nursing homes

  Hotels, bed and breakfasts and serviced accommodation in certain cases

  Marine berths

  Prisons

- Regulated Collective Investments such as Unit Trusts, OEICS and ICVC's

- Gilts

- Bonds

- Fixed Interest stocks

- Investment Trusts

- Direct Quoted Equities

- Trustee Investment Plans
- Loan back to the sponsoring employer
- Equities
- Futures and options traded on recognised futures exchange
- Authorised UK unit Trusts and OEICs and other UCITS funds
- Unauthorised unit Trusts that don't invest in residential property
- Investment Trusts subject to FCA regulation
- Unitised insurance funds from EU insurers and IPAs
- Intangible assets such as intellectual property (IP)
- Deposits and deposit interests
- Traded endowment policies
- Derivative products such as a Contract for difference (CFD)
- Gold bullion
- Peer to peer (P2P) Lending/Crowd Funding
- Off shore funds
- Cash deposits
- Image rights
- Copyrights
- Trademarks

Some of these investment areas may have caveats to them on how they may be allowable - some are only applicable to the UK for instance. It is always appropriate to seek sound advice from your financial advisor or tax advisor when reviewing new investments, ensuring that you stay clear of any potential for tax penalties or loss of tax efficiency.

CALIBRE© Model

To truly understand the huge potential of a SSAS pension one needs to explore the applicable benefits and their very significant impact for you, and the ones you hold dear.

I want to reveal to you the roadmap towards a truly enabled SSAS.

I have run multiple organisations across many countries and continents over the last 27 years, leading large teams of people delivering excellence and resilience in some of the most demanding market sectors such as data centres, energy and engineering. I understand the importance of professionalism and a high-performance culture in everything I set out to achieve.

Operating your SSAS in many ways is no different and the responsibility it requires, the attention to detail and compliance as well as the optimising of the potential, will be directly proportional to your ability to manage it effectively.

A SSAS can offer to those able to harness its power, the missing link to drawing together their entire personal economy and **CREATING EXTRAORDINARY LEVELS OF COMPOUNDING WEALTH** to levels of unprecedented calibre.

The word Calibre is synonymous with quality and exemplary achievement. Take the incredible talent, innovation and precision in Horology, the study of watchmaking. Calibre is the term used for the inner workings or movement of the watch, as opposed to the protective casing. As an engineer I have always been drawn to the precision excellence of the design and manufacture of a watch calibre. Within the hallowed halls of the premium brands of horological royalty such as Patek Philippe, Rolex, Audemars Piguet, Breguet and A. Lange & Sohne, there lies the crème de la crème of precision design and engineering. Simply stunning.

The same level of superlative and exceptional performance can be held within the calibre of a person, organisation or process.

The Collins English dictionary definition of Calibre is:

- The calibre of a person is the quality or standard of their ability or intelligence

- The calibre of something is its quality

It is only fitting that the CALIBRE© MODEL defines the 7 core powers in deploying a SSAS with life changing and multi-generational impact. They are:

C - **Collaborate**

A - **Acquire**

L - **Loan**

I - **Invest**

B - **Borrow**

R - **Resonate**

E - **Educate**

The CALIBRE© Model

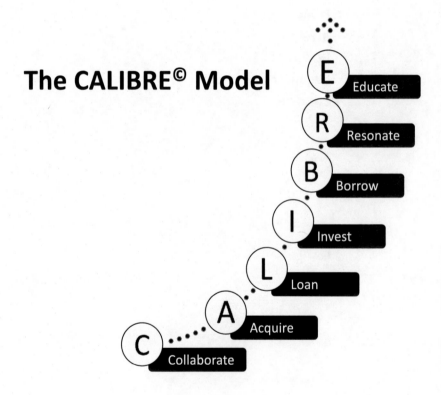

To help you unlock and harness the power of SSAS we will take each of these in turn.

Collaborate

There is an African proverb which has resonated with me for several decades.

"If you want to go fast, go alone. If you want to go far, go together."

This proverb captures much of the essence of a SSAS for many and at multiple levels. This includes of course, the decision to establish a SSAS in the first place and with whom.

As SSAS Trustees we are establishing value – we are the catalyst and our actions have the opportunity to set our own culture. We call this 'creating shared value.'

There is something incredibly powerful and engaging in operating your SSAS where you can not only look after the primary interests of the Trustees, but also create shared value for all stakeholders in the investment process. This might be in the case of investing in a company or undertaking a loan to another entity etc. Remember in the eyes of the law each entity is separate and a legal entity in their own right; this also provides you the ability to retain enormous and compounding value in your own personal economy.

One of the greatest pleasures I have since leaving corporate life at the age of 45 is the freedom to have the choice of who I spend my time with.

As Trustees, few of us have decided to take control of our pensions via a SSAS and thus create a full-time job for ourselves. However, what is particularly liberating is sharing the journey of learning and accountability with other like-minded SSAS Trustees, investigating opportunity and collaborating to enable significant value and reducing risk.

Acquire - **Commercial Property**

The good news is that SSAS's give you a lot of flexibility to invest in a wide range of commercial properties and land. Allowable properties include hotels, care homes, some residential properties with commercial use, student halls, prisons and many more.

Commercial property and importantly, we're talking only about commercial and not residential property, is another popular investment option.

If you choose to invest in commercial property alongside other investments, then you are diversifying and spreading risk. The rent you receive grows tax-free, as does the growth in value of the property. As the property is not owned by the individual, or by the company, it is in most cases ring-fenced from creditors.

Consider this scenario: your pension invests in the property from which your company operates and although your company pays a commercial rent, this rent would be benefiting your pension rather than a third-party landlord.

Your pension can also raise money via a commercial mortgage of up to half of the scheme's net value to help extend the pension's buying power.

If the Commercial Property is to be used by a connected party to the scheme, once it is in the Pension Scheme, the tenant must pay the market rate for the Property and will have to have a formal lease in place.

A business looking to raise cash could sell the property to the scheme. The property, once sold, allows the members/directors of the business to retain assets in the scheme. If there are insufficient funds available within the SSAS, the Trustees can borrow up to 50% of the net value of the SSAS's funds to buy the property. The Trustees take on the borrowing, which is not reflected in the employer's accounts. The property held by the scheme is typically leased to the business at normal commercial terms. The growth in the value of the property is free from Capital Gains Tax and Income Tax.

The Trustees may borrow money from lenders to enable them to purchase particular assets, or to otherwise benefit the SSAS. The maximum the SSAS can borrow is 50% of the net fund value at the date of the loan.

In property investment language this would be assessed on the basis of each individual property with your lender, typically a bank. They would use a ratio of loan to value (LTV) in assessing the leverage or mortgage as it is often referred to, that they would loan on the property.

For example:

A SSAS wishing to acquire a commercial property with an offer accepted of £240,000 could secure a 50% loan to value from a bank. The bank would take first charge on the property as the SSAS owns it. In simple terms (and excluding fees etc) this would mean that the bank would loan £120,000 and the SSAS would use £120,000 of its cash.

To do this the SSAS would have to have a valuation of at least £240,000, given the 50% leverage limit.

Note that the limitation of leverage is on the SSAS fund value and not the property. Technically speaking, as long as the SSAS is large enough, the loan to value on the property could be, say, 60%, as long as the bank would be willing to lend to a SSAS on this basis.

Using the same example as before, if the property was being bought for £240,000 and the bank loaned 60% which would be £144,000 thus requiring the SSAS to use £24,000 less cash at now £96,000. This would be permissible as long as the SSAS had a fund valuation of at least £288,000.

This example is for illustration purposes only to demonstrate how the moving parts operate and what is in the art of the possible - you should be acutely aware that whilst leverage is extremely powerful, it can also harbour risks for the unwary.

Increasing leverage too high can put stress on any property, due to higher interest charges from lenders due to increased risk profile, increased costs, reduced 'head room' in the deal and less contingency in case of a market correction, amongst many others.

It is possible to fund residential development using your SSAS, but there are very specific complications with which you need to familiarise yourself. The key words in that last sentence are FUND and DEVELOPMENT. What the sentence did NOT say was that you can own residential property – you simply cannot and must not in a SSAS!

The frequent question I am often asked is "what are my options in funding a residential development?".

Let us assume one owns a commercial office building in the SSAS. This has now secured the benefit of planning permission or permitted development rights to convert to residential apartments. How can the SSAS undertake this development?

Firstly, let us restate the golden rule. A SSAS cannot own residential property (and this also includes the freehold rights to leasehold residential property by the way).

There are two main choices that you have:

a. The SSAS sells the commercial property to a development company (which could be wholly owned by you), raises development finance and undertakes the development right from the start in an industry recognised structure – see my book "Commercial to Residential Conversions: the essential manual for property developers" for details on how to do this.

b. The SSAS proceeds to develop the property towards residential use. However, at the point where services are connected and kitchens and bathrooms are installed, the building will gain building control sign off and will be at the point of certificate of inhabitation. BEFORE this point the SSAS must have sold the property.

Now if you have ever tried to sell a partially completed development you may recognise the difficulty on raising funding from banks, transferring structural building warranties etc and instead may wish to consider number 1 above, as a more straight forward option.

As I have mentioned before, the ability to lay one's head on the pillow at night and sleep easy is a blessing and something to cherish. I personally prefer to keep things simple, attract low rates of interest and commence developments with a high probability of assured outcomes.

Imagine some hypothetical scenarios which can further allow the creative ideas to be gathered well in advance of retirement age to provide many options for your future wealth creation:

Scenario 1: Your SSAS holds a commercial property which has just obtained residential planning permission. It could take steps to convert the property into residential dwellings but sell the properties off plan (prior to completion) to third parties - even to yourself personally or a company you own, as long as an independent valuation is obtained providing evidence of market value.

Scenario 2: Your SSAS holds a commercial property, for which you have received planning permission to convert into a block of flats. As you are over 55, you are entitled to draw a tax-free lump sum from your pension of up to 25% of the total fund value. Instead of drawing cash, you transfer the commercial property from your SSAS into your private ownership.

Next, you transfer the property from your personal ownership to your company as a director's loan. It is permissible to loan money from your SSAS to your business to fund the residential development of your commercial property.

Why is this so tax-efficient? Interest on the SSAS loan is tax deductible for your business but received tax-free in the SSAS. In short: you effectively benefit from an interest-free loan while helping to boost your pension fund, all the while freeing up the money needed to fund your residential development to sell on at a profit in your personal hands.

You can also use your SSAS to buy land that has been zoned for residential development. This is a permissible investment as long as the land does not contain any building or structure that is suitable for use as a dwelling. You could then obtain residential planning permission and sell the land onto a developer.

Loan

SSAS schemes can make loans to unconnected unquoted UK companies but loans to members (or those connected to members) are not permitted other than a loan by a SSAS to a sponsoring employer.

Obviously seek expert advice as always, however the simple test to remember here is are you connected in any way via these two tests:

1. In Blood: are you related through family – brother, sister, husband, wife, children etc

2. In Business: co-director or shareholder

A SSAS can lend money to the sponsoring employer providing 5 key criteria are met:

1. **Amount**: up to 50% of the fund can be loaned

2. **Term**: can be from 1 year up to a maximum term of no more than 5 years

3. **Basis of loan**: Must be on a repayment basis consisting of equal repayments of capital and interest monthly, quarterly or annually over the term.

4. **Security**: the loan must be secured by a first charge on a suitable asset which has at least the equivalent value to the loan plus interest, as well as some additional upside depending on the asset.

5. **Interest**: the minimum interest rate a scheme can charge is calculated at a minimum of 1% above the average of the base lending rates of 6 high street banks.

In summary in order for the loan to be compliant, it must be on the basis that it is Prudent, Secure and Commercial.

Investment Convention

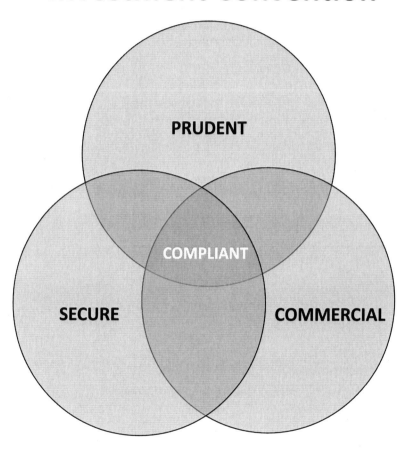

When considering any basis for a loan, including loan security, it would be prudent to consider yourself as the bank when making the loan. For those familiar with banks loaning on a property, where they take the first charge at Land Registry as security, let us consider their risk management strategy.

Would a bank loan £100,000 on the basis of a first charge on a property valued at open market value of £100,000? The answer is a resounding 'no' as any property investor will testify!

Risk is all around us and forms part of any investors (SSAS Trustee or otherwise) due diligence. It is for this reason that I always refer to this as bank grade due diligence as you must adopt a position of bank grade levels of integrity and research to protect your capital.

A bank may consider a number of factors that could affect the property value such as market rises and falls, shifts in the local demographics and area and local events that might affect property prices etc.

Hence one might typically expect a 70% – 80% Loan to Value (LTV) to be applied to a loan.

Loan Example 1

Let us take a 75% loan to value approach on a £100,000 loan with a 5% interest rate over 5 years.

Considerations:

- Does the loan fall within the 50% of fund value rule? Yes, proceed

- Is the term between 1 and 5 years? Yes, proceed

- Is the interest above the minimum 1% rule? Yes, proceed

- Minimum security required:

  o Capital sum: £100,000

  o Interest: (Year 1: 5% x £100,000) + (Year 2: 5% x £80,000)

+ (Year 3: 5% x £60,000) + (Year 4: 5% x £40,000) + (Year 5: 5% x £20,000) = £15,000

- o Security: 75% Loan to Value
- o Total security required: (£100,000 + £15,000)/75*100 = £153,333

Loan Example 2

Let us take an 80% loan to value approach on a £100,000 loan with a 3% interest rate over 2 years.

Considerations:

- Does the loan fall within the 50% of fund value rule? Yes, proceed

- Is the term between 1 and 5 years? Yes, proceed

- Is the interest above the minimum 1% rule? Yes, proceed

- Minimum security required:
  - o Capital sum: £100,000
  - o Interest: (Year 1: 3% x £100,000) + (Year 2: 3% x £80,000) = £5,400
  - o Security: 80% Loan to Value
  - o Total security required: (£100,000 + £5,400)/80*100 = £131,750

The basis of your loan must be on a commercial basis. We have established the minimum acceptable rate of interest, however what determines the maximum interest rate you could loan on?

The answer lies in simple market forces and is a combination of:

- Market opportunity
- Risk factors
- Competition

- Other available opportunities
- Negotiation

There is no maximum interest rate. However, the overall position will inevitably be dictated on what the economics of the opportunity can ultimately stand, unless other factors are brought into the equation such as time pressure and deal stress on behalf of the opportunity owner. In that case your due diligence must be acutely positioned to understand risk and reward.

Invest

There is no objection by HMRC to a SSAS making loans to third parties i.e. persons not connected to members or sponsoring employers. Such loans are normally on an arm's length basis at a commercial market rate.

No more than 50% of the pension scheme's assets can be invested in shares and/or unsecured loans to unquoted UK companies.

The Trustees can invest up to 5% of the net asset value of the SSAS in shares of a sponsoring company and are further subject to an overall limit of 20% of the net asset value in any such transactions. For example, the SSAS could invest in five sponsoring companies provided they invest no more than 5% in any one company and no more than 20% in total.

It is important to make sure that the SSAS does not inadvertently take an indirect holding of taxable property through an investment into a company which would create a taxable event.

Intellectual property: Intellectual property (IP) can be a key business asset and covers the following:

- Patents
- Trade marks
- Goodwill within a business
- Design types
- Copyright

Valuing intellectual property can be difficult and is generally considered as the 'strength of the IP in the marketplace and financial performance of the IP'.

The choice of valuation methodology will vary on a case by case basis depending on the type of IP asset that is being valued. Once the IP has been assigned to the pension, it must be revalued on a regular basis to maintain the integrity of the IP assets.

The type of due diligence that may be required by a SSAS to properly consider an investment in IP might include:

- What is the brand strength of the business?
- What IP the business currently has and its perceived or valued strength?
- Is the IP registered or unregistered?
- How long has the business been trading?
- A copy of the last three years certified accounts and financial review
- Detailed overview of the business and its day to day operations and future plans. This would also include an appraisal of the prevailing market
- Ownership and operating structure of the business
- Geographical business coverage
- Key competitor analysis

Ideally a brand or IP related business valuation would be undertaken by an ISO 10668 Brand valuation specialist. These organisations focus on the requirements for monetary brand valuation as specified by the International Organisation for Standardisation (ISO) for the procedures and methods of measuring the value of a brand.

As with an asset class it would be prudent to ensure that consideration is only given on a certain loan to value basis. Hence if the IP valuation is £150,000 then you may make an assessment of applying a loan of say 60% which would be £90,000. Think like a bank, do your bank grade due diligence and preserve your capital with a passion!

Gold bullion: Gold can be used to diversify an investment portfolio and investment grade gold bullion is the only physical commodity that can be held within a SSAS pension.

There are a few rules to follow when considering gold bullion, held within a SSAS, which you should familiarise yourself with:

- Investment grade gold bullion has a specific exemption from being 'tangible moveable property' thus allowing it to be held within a SSAS.

- Gold bullion must have a purity of not less than 995 thousandths and held in a form of weight acceptable by the bullion markets.

- Gold bullion cannot be held personally by a Trustee.

- Gold bullion must be held in a secure vault and held to the order of the Trustees.

- Gold bullion is held for investment purposes only and the Trustee must have no use for the gold.

These services provide the required gold storage arrangements and have sufficient controls in place to ensure that any monies are paid back to the pension scheme bank account only.

Due diligence checks will need to be undertaken by the client's financial adviser and before any instruction can be given to the gold bullion dealer.

Gold bullion can be a volatile investment asset with no guarantee of future returns.

Unquoted UK equities: Unquoted or unlisted equities are shares of a private limited company which are not traded on a recognised stock exchange, such as the London Stock Exchange. Generally, investments in UK registered unquoted companies are perfectly acceptable, however not in overseas unquoted trading companies. The maximum amount of shares held overall in unquoted trading companies would be limited to 50% of the value of the SSAS fund valuation.

Borrow - Loan Back

There are many advantages to a SSAS, however one which isn't available with other types of pension is a connected-party loan to your sponsoring employer and this can be a highly beneficial investment.

Put simply, this loan option – which is available to any participating employer in the pension – provides a source of business funding without having to seek investment from a third party, such as a bank. And the beauty of it is you have control and security.

A SSAS can make authorised payments to its sponsoring employer often referred to as a Loan Back. Any payment made outside of the rules set out in The Pension Manual is an unauthorised employer payment and subject to tax consequences.

There are five key tests that a loan must satisfy to qualify as an authorised employer loan (Loan Back). If a loan fails to meet one or more of these tests it will be classified as an unauthorised payment.

The five key tests are

1. security

2. interest rates

3. term of loan

4. maximum amount of loan, and

5. repayment terms.

A loan to a person connected to a member or sponsoring employer, and who is not a member or sponsoring employer, is treated as though the loan were made to the sponsoring employer and must comply with the five tests.

Security

When a SSAS makes a Loan Back to a sponsoring employer the amount of the loan must be secured throughout the full term as a first charge on any asset either owned by the sponsoring employer, or some other entity. At the time the loan is made the security used must be of at least equal value to the face value of the loan including interest.

There must be no other charge on the asset that takes priority over the charge made by the scheme.

If the asset used as security is replaced by another asset, the value of the replacement at the time the security is placed must be at least equal to the lower of:

- the market value of the asset it has replaced, or

- the amount of loan outstanding (including interest)

Interest rate

All Loan Backs made by a SSAS must charge interest at least equivalent to the rate specified in The Registered Pension Schemes (Prescribed Interest Rates for Authorised Employer Loans) Regulations 2005. This is to ensure that a commercial rate of interest is applied to the loan.

The minimum interest rate a scheme may charge is calculated by reference to 1% above the average of the base lending rates of the following 6 leading high street banks specified in the regulations:

- The Bank of Scotland plc

- Barclays Bank plc

- HSBC Bank plc

- Lloyds Bank plc

- National Westminster Bank plc and

- The Royal Bank of Scotland plc.

The average rate calculated should be rounded up as necessary to the nearest multiple of 0.25%.

A registered pension scheme may make a loan at a fixed rate of interest as long as that interest rate is at least the rate specified. As long as the terms of the loan remain unchanged there will be no requirement to alter the interest charged on the loan during its life.

Term of loan

The repayment period of the loan must not be longer than 5 years from the date the loan was made.

An unauthorised payment occurs when the repayment period for a loan is longer than 5 years from the date the loan was made unless the loan has been rolled over in accordance with the requirements for Rollovers.

Maximum amount of loan

A SSAS is restricted to the amount it loans via a Loan Back to 50% of the aggregate of the amount of the cash sums held and the net market value of the assets within the SSAS immediately before the loan is made.

If the Loan Back is made and it is found to exceed the 50% limit, the amount of the Loan Back in excess of the 50% limit is an unauthorised payment.

Repayment terms

All Loan Backs must be repayable as a minimum, in equal instalments of capital and interest for each complete year of the loan, beginning on the date that the loan is made and ending on the last day of the following 12 month period. This is known as a loan year.

The amount of capital and interest repayments payable by the end of each loan year must not be less than 'the required amount' however it can be more which is perfectly acceptable. The Loan Back is calculated as follows:

[(L+TIP) / TLY] x NLY

Where:

L is the amount of the loan

TIP is the total interest payable

TLY is the total number of loan years

NLY is the number of loan years in the period

Rollovers

Rules for Loan Backs does acknowledge that on occasions the sponsoring employer may encounter issues with making the repayments. Where an employer is having genuine difficulties making repayments and there is an amount of capital or interest outstanding at the end of the Loan Back period, the Loan Back period can be extended or "rolled over" for a period up to a further 5 years.

A loan may only be rolled over once. If a loan is rolled over more than once then the Unauthorised Payments tax rules will apply. The rollover loan will not be treated as a new loan and therefore any existing security may continue, even if the security is less than the face value of the loan. Any increase to the original loan will be treated as a new loan. The 50% limit will only be re-tested in the event of a new loan being taken out.

Case Study – First Charge

Let us take an example of Mrs & Mrs Arnold who have worked their entire adult lives watching the pennies and saving. They have contributed into a combination of state and company pensions and are now retired, living off a monthly annuity pension amounting to £220 in total.

During their working life they purchased their family home and always harboured the ambition to pay off the mortgage which they duly achieved before they both retired.

Their daughter Jane is a SSAS Trustee and property investor having left her legal career at the age of 40. Jane wanted to enable her property company, which is also the sponsoring company of the SSAS, to borrow £150,000 via a Loan Back from her SSAS. In order to provide the relevant security for this, Jane's property company needed to provide a first charge at Land Registry which it did not have as the portfolio had mortgages on (the first charge being taken by the respective mortgage companies).

Jane's parents had indicated to her that they were struggling to live the life they wanted to, due to monetary constraints. They wanted to travel, to see parts of the world they had always wanted to see; they had taken up hobbies and needed more cash in their personal economy.

In summary they were asset rich and cash poor and didn't know how to change their financial outlook.

Jane suggested that the available first charge on her parent's house, with a current market valuation of £300,000, was something that would be useful to support her business and in return could provide a return for her parents.

Jane discussed this sensitively with her parents, whom she had enjoyed a long and trusting relationship with. Jane had plans that the £150,000 would be used to invest in the next stage growth and working capital requirements of her business. She did her calculations and offered a £200 fee per month in return for the first charge, for a period of five years which was the duration of the loan back. This fee would be payable via a contract between Jane's property company and her parents.

Jane decided that the overall cost of the 'fee' for the first charge facility of £12,000 plus a small amount of legal costs to establish the first charge and to remove it at the end of the term, was great value for her to secure the Loan Back.

This is how the final transaction played out:

Property value:	£300,000
Security for Loan required:	£150,000
Max Loan to Value:	75%
Security required:	First charge at Land Registry
Beneficiary of first charge security:	SSAS Trust

Maximum loan security possible:	£300,000 x 75% = £225,000
Actual loan security achieved:	£150,000/£300,000 x 100 = 50%
Property company fee to parents:	£200 pcm = £2,400 pa = £12,000 over 5-year term

From Jane's property company perspective, they would be entering into a Loan Back contract as sponsoring company to the SSAS Trust based on a 5-year term where they would be paying capital, plus interest back each year over the term.

Jane explained to her parents that the initial loan to value security on the property, whilst commencing at 50%, would technically be reducing as follows over the following 5 years until the first charge is removed, once the loan is repaid in full at year 5:

- Year 0   Loan to value 50%

- Year 1   Loan to value 40%

- Year 2   Loan to value 30%

- Year 3   Loan to value 20%

- Year 4   Loan to value 10%

- Year 5   Loan fully re-paid and first charge removed

Note: Loan Back interest was agreed at 3% in line with HMRC approval guidelines of a minimum of 1% above the average of 6 high street lenders base rates. The interest exposure has not been calculated, however in reality you would include that as a liability also, until fully repaid.

First Charge Enablement

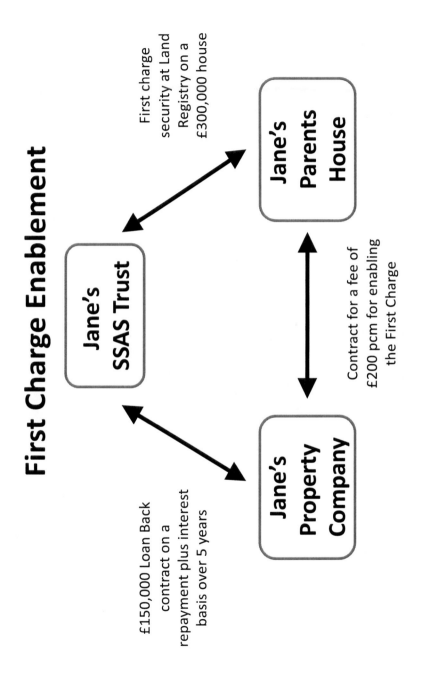

First charge security at Land Registry on a £300,000 house

Jane's Parents House

Jane's SSAS Trust

Contract for a fee of £200 pcm for enabling the First Charge

Jane's Property Company

£150,000 Loan Back contract on a repayment plus interest basis over 5 years

Resonate

For many who have had pensions throughout their employment careers, the pension funds may not have always felt tangible or real even and may not have truly resonated as active investments.

One SSAS Trustee described the feeling of finally securing their £400,000 transfer of their funds like they had created money out of thin air! Of course, this statement was entirely based around the tangibility and feeling of closeness and control rather than a lack of respect, but it really resonated with me. That priceless feeling of joy, responsibility, excitement, accountability, passion and ownership all melded together to form a hugely powerful genesis for a multi-generational investment vehicle.

Some may have only ever taken a cursory look at an annual pension statement at the end of each year with any active pension management limited to a hope that the next year will change the funds fortunes!

Now with a SSAS everything becomes real and vivid. You are in control of your pension funds in their entirety!!

You can read your bank balance on the bank account App on your smart phone.

Of course, with this comes the accountability of knowing that no-one else is going to do this for you. You are the master of your ship and you will be plotting your course.

This directly engaging feeling resonates with many Trustees, myself included, knowing that the accountability and responsibility rest with the decisions we make.

The duty of care to your funds and, if applicable, to our fellow Trustees is one of significant importance and should not be taken lightly. With due diligence that you might take in establishing any legal entity with shareholders and directors, you will have selected a great Trustee fit to embrace the combined skills and risk & reward philosophy between the Trustees.

This active engagement resonating across the SSAS Trustee

framework further enhances the appeal, accountability and long-term planning that starts with a clear plan and the excitement of making those first and important steps towards controlling the final aspects of your personal economy after so many years.

This new responsibility placed on the newly created Trustee places a burden of responsibility. However, of all the Trustees I have met I struggle to think of a single person who has taken this responsibility lightly. The manner in which a SSAS Trust resonates with Trustees and their family unit is incredible powerful and wonderous to see who it proliferates in many different ways.

Educate

The responsibility of operating a SSAS, like any investment strategy, comes with an important need to educate oneself in how to operate the SSAS in a compliant and optimised manner.

Remember that naivety is no excuse to HMRC. If you meander over the tax guidelines and stray into non-compliant territory, you will incur substantial tax penalties. In fact meandering is no way of operating a SSAS in the same way you would not wish to operate any other legal entity - limited company, limited liability partnership (LLP) or charity etc.

This is why we have established the SSAS Alliance to enhance education, knowledge, collaboration and connection between Trustees and the availability, detail and understanding available to all to ensure optimised confidence, performance and progression of all SSAS Alliance members.

More about SSAS Alliance in a later chapter or find us at www.ssasalliance.com.

Of the thousands of SSAS connections that I have made over recent years through SSAS Alliance, and also being a developer and Trustee myself, there is a consistent attribute shared by almost all Trustees and those interested in SSAS Trusteeship.

That is the unquenchable thirst and desire to learn, experience, educate, share, collaborate and progress at each step along the way. There is something inherently satisfying in growing personally in every aspect and meeting wonderful people along the way who share the same passion and who are delighted to explore collaboration and creating shared value.

"We are only competing with what we are capable of" - Mark Stokes, Chairman and co-founder of SSAS Alliance.

Another important aspect of education that I see Trustees often sharing with a passion is that of educating their future generations as well as themselves.

Many of us strive towards leaving an amazing and rewarding legacy for our children and to do that we are aware that we must ensure that we have suitably equipped them with the skills, personal attributes and understanding to carry our legacy forward. To best enable them to advance the great work we have achieved during our life time they are going to need to be trained and experienced to take the legacy to the next level, facing different challenges and seizing on new and exciting opportunities that may arise in an ever changing and connected world.

This will, in part, enable deep rooted foundations ensuring, as far as possible, that our vision for a multi-generational legacy will grow and prosper and become increasingly resilient over time, embracing the new and dynamic future of our ever-changing world.

Genuinely Diverse Commercial Vehicles

If a SSAS holds an indirect interest in taxable property by investing in a vehicle that has any interest in taxable property and the vehicle is not a Genuinely Diverse Commercial Vehicle, the investment will give rise to tax charges.

This could happen if the SSAS purchases shares or makes a loan to the vehicle which has interests in what would be taxable property if it were held in the SSAS.

The important consideration here is that the entity must be a

Genuinely Diverse Commercial Vehicle.

These vehicles can include:

- Trading companies/concerns

- Investment companies/special purpose vehicles

- Other collective investment schemes including unit Trusts, open ended investment companies and UK REITS

- Individuals

A vehicle is a Genuinely Diverse Commercial Vehicle if it, and the investment in it, satisfy the following criteria, not only when the SSAS makes the investment but all the time that it holds that investment.

Where the vehicle is trading:

- The vehicle's main activity is the carrying on of a trade, profession or vocation

- The SSAS Trustee, either alone or together with associated persons do not have control of the vehicle

- Neither the SSAS Trustee nor a person connected with the Trustee is a controlling director of the vehicle or any other vehicle which holds an interest in the vehicle directly or indirectly

- The SSAS does not hold an interest in the vehicle to allow a Trustee or a person connected with a Trustee to occupy or use taxable property

A controlling director is a person who is a director or manger and is either on their own or with others, a beneficial owner of, or able, directly or indirectly, to control 20% or more of the ordinary share capital of the company.

24. CASE STUDY: COMMERCIAL PROPERTY

"90% of all millionaires become so through owning real estate"

Andrew Carnegie

In mid 2018, my fellow Trustee, Nigel Greene identified a wonderful commercial property in Colchester, Essex which consisted of five commercial properties under a single title. The property was located in the old part of Colchester, the oldest City in England by all accounts, and was set just off a highly desirable cobbled High Street, popular with boutique retail shops and service industries such as estate agents and café's, all with considerable footfall.

Optimised Compounded Investments

@

Portal Precinct, Colchester

The properties consist as follows:

a. Commercial lease for a café with several years remaining on the lease.

b. Tattoo parlour with 3 months remaining on its lease. Nigel and I resisted the urge to have matching tattoos to celebrate!!

c. Vacant shop.

d. Vacant dance studio/shop.

e. Clothing repair business with 2 years remaining on the lease.

The property was in a position where, with our specialist knowledge of commercial property, we saw the potential to drive significant value and appreciation into this asset.

The two diagrams that follow show how we have secured and developed multiple phases of additional value that will serve our families for decades to come. It really is that powerful!

3 Stage Transaction (after initial purchase)

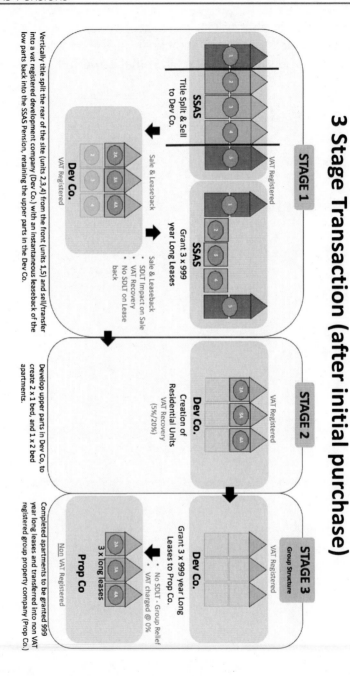

STAGE 1

VAT Registered

SSAS
Title Split & Sell
to Dev Co.

Sale & Leaseback

Dev Co.
VAT Registered

SSAS
Grant 3 x 999
year Long Leases

Sale & Leaseback
* SDLT Impact on Sale
* VAT Recovery
* No SDLT on Lease
  back

Vertically title split the rear of the site (units 2,3,4) from the front (units 1,5) and sell/transfer into a vat registered development company (Dev Co.) with an instantaneous leaseback of the low parts back into the SSAS Pension, retaining the upper parts in the Dev Co.

STAGE 2

VAT Registered

Dev Co.
Creation of
Residential Units
VAT Recovery
(5%/20%)

Develop upper parts in Dev Co, to create 2 x 1 bed, and 1 x 2 bed apartments.

STAGE 3
Group Structure

VAT Registered

Dev Co.
Grant 3 x 999 year Long
Leases to Prop Co.

* No SDLT - Group Relief
* VAT charged @ 0%

Non VAT Registered

Prop Co
3 x long leases

Completed apartments to be granted 999 year long leases and transferred into non VAT registered group property company (Prop Co.)

Final Structure and Funding

SSAS

VAT Registered

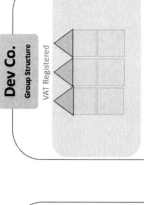

✓ SSAS to grant occupational leases to incoming tenants.

✓ Commercial funding up to 50% LTV to replenish SSAS balance.

✓ Long term rental income, cash flow and equity growth in highly efficient tax vehicle

Dev Co.
Group Structure

VAT Registered

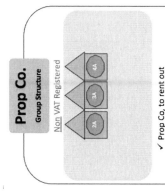

✓ Dev Co. holding freehold interest for commercial units 2,3,4 and residential units 2a,3a,4a.

✓ Collection of annual ground rents (subject to VAT).

Prop Co.
Group Structure

Non VAT Registered

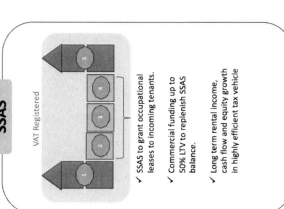

✓ Prop Co, to rent out apartments on AST's

✓ BTL lending between 55%/60% to repay all costs.

✓ Long term rental income / cash flow and equity growth.

The following identifies the key steps in the process that complement the diagrams to give you a really deep dive into how knowledge, experience and action can come together to achieve great things:

1. Our accepted offer of £620,000 was fully conditional on securing planning permission.

2. We identified that the 3 vacant units could have their 'uppers' at first floor level converted to residential units.

3. Full planning permission was required due to the stunning location being in a conservation area, hence Permitted Development Rights did not apply.

4. We duly applied for full planning permission which was granted.

5. We then completed on the purchase of the property in the SSAS in cash on this particular occasion.

6. We then title split units 2,3,4 and sold them into our Development Company for development into 3 residential apartments as well as the 3 commercial properties below.

7. We then sold the 999 year virtual freehold interests of the commercial units back to the SSAS in a quasi-sale and leaseback.

8. We then developed the residential units into 3 beautifully appointed 1 & 2 bedroom apartments. Note that these are now importantly outside of our SSAS, in our development company.

9. The development company collects the ground rent for the 3 commercial units with a 999 year lease each year.

10. As a development company it is VAT registered and can therefore reclaim the VAT paid on professional fees (20%) and on the main contractors build costs (5%).

11. Once completed, the residential units were then sold into a Property Company where they will be held long-term. This is a non-VAT registered entity as we do not want to charge VAT to our tenants on AST rents.

12. The Property Company raised Buy to Let finance on the purchase of the 3 residential units.

13. Commercial units 1 & 5 remain in the SSAS and have 10-15 year FRI leases placed on them with counter parties with very reasonable covenant strengths.

14. Units 2,3 & 4 have 10-15 year FRI leases placed on them with counter parties with very reasonable covenant strengths.

15. Units 1 - 5 were then re-financed on the strength of the improved leases.

16. The re-finance replenished the funds of the SSAS and enabled yet further investment opportunity.

17. All freehold and leasehold commercial units as well as the residential units are held in their respective legal entities in perpetuity.

As Warren Buffet said, "Our favourite holding period is forever".

Incidentally, I met Warren Buffet and had lunch with him in 1992 in Omaha, Nebraska… but that story will have to wait for another day I am afraid!

This SINGLE investment cluster will provide our Trustees and families with:

    a.   5 commercial units within our SSAS with ever increasingly secured leases for long term cashflow for decades to come.

    b.   3 residential apartments which will be held in our Property Company for strong monthly cashflow and long-term capital appreciation in this desirable area.

    c.   3 commercial unit freeholds held in our Development Company.

This asset is a unique and extremely valuable case study of establishing multiple layers of compounding wealth and how a SSAS can be the catalyst for that value creation.

The first layer of compounding sits in the SSAS that has benefitted from driven appreciation through planning permission, sale of the units 2, 3 & 4 and renegotiating the leases on more favourable terms, as and when they come up for renewal.

The second layer of compounding sits outside of the SSAS but has been directly ENABLED by the SSAS. This represents 3 residential units and 3 commercial unit freeholds.

How can you gain FIVE layers of compounding wealth across your portfolio of interests using your SSAS as a catalyst for growth? These may well include, like ours:

- SSAS cashflow
- SSAS asset capital growth
- Property company cashflow
- Property company asset capital growth
- Development company freeholds and their potential

An amazing deal I think you will agree, for 10-12 months of hard effort and a heap of tenacity!!

25. ONE PART OF OUR STRATEGY

**"It is not the strongest of the species that survives, nor the most intelligent that survives.
It is the one that is most adaptable to change"**

Charles Darwin

Following the success of Portal Precinct in our previous case study, I want to share with you what this type of catalytic strategy can truly achieve on a rolling strategy of securing only ONE more asset of a similar nature, each year, for the next 5 years.

That would provide a portfolio of asset classes based on the compounded year on year illustration shown here of the potential return from the introduction of a similar new asset each year.

Example: Portal Precinct + 5 Year Strategy

	£ Starting	£ Ending	Growth%
YR1	1,000,000	1,207,337	21%
YR2	1,207,337	1,302,312	30%
	1,302,312	1,509,650	51%
YR3	1,509,650	1,606,494	61%
	1,606,494	1,701,469	70%
	1,701,469	1,908,806	91%
YR4	1,908,806	2,007,602	101%
	2,007,602	2,104,446	110%
	2,104,446	2,199,421	120%
	2,199,421	2,406,759	141%
YR5	2,406,759	2,501,734	150%
	2,501,734	2,598,579	160%
	2,598,579	2,693,553	169%
	2,693,553	2,786,098	179%
	2,786,098	**2,993,435**	199%
Growth		**1,993,435**	**199%**

Compounded year on year illustration of the potential return from the introduction of a new asset each calender year.

Based on a SSAS starting position of £1,000,000 that could grow to £2,993,435 representing a 199% growth rate over 5 years AND more importantly, setting in motion a juggernaut of multigenerational compounding that will continue for decades.

Quite impressive I think you will agree.

So that you do not just see the upside, please note that there are risks of course which you must assess, as indeed we have, such as:

• Void tenancies which we have allocated contingency against.

• Capital growth rates being inconsistent over longer term trends.

• Interest rate volatility.

• Commercial lease defaults.

Remember this strategy is only mapped out for the next 5 years. Just imagine what the following 20 years might look.

Let us now assume that we do nothing more for the following 20 years (after the initial 5 years) apart from holding those assets, retaining the cashflow and sitting tight.

Can you imagine the capital growth mounting up, with no re-financing? The loan to value would gradually sink to a tiny percentage, the equity would build up handsomely and rental values would increase substantially, albeit our mortgage costs would remain fairly sedentary (assuming no major increase in interest rates).

Alternatively, we could take a view to re-finance every 3-5 years over the next 20 years. Each time we could maximise our loan to value financing and release the equity and re-invest through our SSAS or our Property company, thus further enhancing the compounding.

Now, let us further compound that by:

1. Continuing to do a single development each year for 25 years.

2. Every 3-5 years refinance to a moderate loan to value.

3. Reinvest equity release in a further series of investments.

4. Rinse and repeat.

5. Rinse and repeat etc.

I will refrain from showing you the numbers on that calculation but a single word sprins to mind. Exponential.

However, I think we can all agree that at that stage there are only first world problems in your SSAS and business interests. You will then have opportunity, resilience and legacy as a result of extremely substantial levels of compounding wealth and a very significant array of options stretching ahead of you.

Your SSAS represents a gateway to a whole new world of options available to you in so many diverse fields.

This is just one of the many investment options you could take, and I have tried to keep it simple to illustrate that it does not have to be incredibly complex to achieve amazing results. Other investment options can be inter-woven to create resilience and diversity of course.

The possibilities are almost infinite as long as you abide by the three basic rules:

- Never lose money/capital.

- Always add value.

- Always stay compliant - do not burden yourself with the pressure and pain of unnecessary tax charges.

26. CASE STUDY: PLANNING GAIN

"The biggest competition is with me. I am not looking to follow others or pull them down. I'm planning to test my own boundaries"

Rain

Wright Street in Hull is on the fringe of the vibrant business and commercial centre of Kingston upon Hull. In 2016 our Trustees identified a row of three, five-storey Georgian terraces which were previously the offices of an accountancy practice.

The accountancy practice had been sold to a larger practice and the building had been vacant for almost three years before coming to the market - we swiftly reviewed the potential acquisition of the asset for our SSAS.

The building was Grade II listed and benefitted from a number of beautiful period features throughout the property, which in Hull, following the extensive and devastating bombing during World War II, are particularly treasured assets within the local community.

We acquired the asset within our SSAS on a conditional basis, subject to gaining full planning permission to convert some, or all, of the previously B1A office accommodation to residential C3 use class. It was considered an opportunity to enhance the value of the property at a relatively minor cost to the SSAS, prior to engaging any bank finance. It also opened out other options for us in the future other than its current commercial use, which was our primary strategy.

For those of you who are developers (or may have read my book 'Commercial to Residential Conversions: the essential manual for property developers') you may recall that Permitted Development Rights applies to B1A use class conversion to C3. However, in this case the property was Grade II listed and hence required full planning permission.

During the 12-month conditional exchange period we prepared and submitted the planning application for conversion of the commercial property to 18, 1 and 2 bedroom apartments of exquisite quality in a desirable area.

Once planning permission was granted, we duly completed on the purchase of the commercial property in our SSAS.

At this stage we had 3 options for consideration:

1. **Lease:** Secure a commercial lease with a strong covenanted tenant, possibly on a 10-15 years full repair and insuring (FRI) lease basis. We undertook commercial soft market testing in the area and significant due diligence noting the recent and on-going changes in the area, whilst we secured planning. We decided that recent gentrification of the local area lent the property more towards residential than commercial use at this stage.

2. **Develop**: Develop the property towards residential use as per the planning application. I must stress the word 'towards' as it is very clear for all SSAS Trustees that they must not own residential units in their Trust, given that commercial property moves to residential use at the point of certified habitation (i.e. bathroom, kitchen and all services commissioned and passed for habitation). Importantly this would have meant that the SSAS would have had to have sold prior to this point, which would be a building site still – being still a couple of months from completion. Can you imagine asking a bank to fund a partially completed asset? Our risk management policy meant that we were uncomfortable with putting into place this kind of funding structure on a technically incomplete asset.

3. **Sell**: Sell the property from the SSAS to a development special purpose vehicle (SPV), which was a limited company in this case, and proceed as is common place in raising traditional commercial and development finance to complete the development and sell the completed apartments.

Investment
Planning
Gain

@

Wright Street,
Hull

We decided to sell the commercial property from the SSAS to our development company (option 3) which gave clarity to everyone in the process and left very little room for uncertainty.

One of the important considerations in any investment decision you make is the ability for you to lay your head on the pillow at night and sleep easy. We did not want the stress of having to raise finance on a partially completed asset, as an example, so chose a readily fundable, simple and well understood option and were delighted that the development was fully completed as planned.

One area you should be careful of is to ensure that your SSAS does not fall foul of becoming a trading entity that, for the purposes of this example, buys property, gains planning uplift and sells on for a profit on a repeated basis. You should seek advice from your SSAS administrator and be acutely aware that you do not step outside of the guidelines and become liable for punitive tax charges.

27. WHAT CAN A SSAS NOT DO?

"...but in this world, nothing can be said to be certain, except death and taxes"

Benjamin Franklin

Rather than say what a SSAS cannot do, it is technically more accurate to identify what investments and activities will become taxable events and thus loosing the tax efficiencies of a SSAS.

I thought very carefully about each of the quotes in the chapter headings and the one in this chapter by Benjamin Franklin "but in this world, nothing can be said to be certain, except death and taxes" more than most. I only partially agree with this quote so have included it to provoke debate and thought.

None of us wish to pay tax naively and without due cause or obligation and none of us, I believe, genuinely wish to pay less tax than is due. The choice we have is to fully investigate how we can use the processes and systems as they have been laid out and intend to be used by HMRC. Compliance is everything, as is resourcefulness.

In the UK, HMRC lay the tax rules down very clearly and we, the tax payer, surely have the requirement to seek great counsel and advice to pay the correct amount of tax for the given circumstances and environment. A SSAS or a limited company are two great examples of us creating the circumstances and environment to enable us to have a tax optimised position.

I have never 'nickel and dimed' on great advice, rather seeking instead to build up a great array of counsel, knowledge and wisdom that can be brought to bear to ensure that each decision, investment or deployment is undertaken with compliance, risk management and tax efficiency in mind.

There is a huge diversity of what a SSAS Trustee can consider for their investment strategy and equally there are key guidelines that must be followed to ensure economic viability, tax efficiency and overall compliance. A SSAS can do many things, however stepping over the guidelines and rules will trigger investigations and potentially result in serious tax penalties.

For example - investments currently permitted by primary legislation but subsequently made subject to heavy tax penalties, therefore rendering them uninvestable, include:

- Any item of tangible moveable property
- Exotic assets like:

    vintage cars

    yachts

    wine

    stamps

    antique furniture

    works of art

    rare books

    oriental rugs

- Residential property
- Plant and machinery:

    wind turbines

    solar panels

- Commodities
- Personal loans directly, or indirectly, to Trustees or persons connected with a Trustee
- Investments considered to be personal chattels
- Unsecured loans to the sponsoring employer
- Overseas unquoted equities
- Off-plan hotel rooms
- Carbon credits
- Cloud lending
- Land banking
- Storage pods
- Any taxable movable property (with a market value that does

not exceed £6,000)

- Gold Krugerrands
- Loans to member Trustees or their families
- Jewellery and gemstones

Property is one of the most popular asset classes that SSAS Trustees may decide to consider so we will review this separately and in more granular detail below.

There are a number of properties that cannot be accepted within a SSAS or in a tax efficient way (excluding penalty tax considerations):

- Residential property is not permitted under any circumstances.

- Student accommodation. An exception to this rule might be where the student accommodation is directly connected to an educational establishment.

- Commercial property with a residential element. For example, a retail shop with a flat above may only be accepted if it can be clearly demonstrated that the residential element is an integral part of the commercial property and not a separate use class under planning classification.

- Commercial freeholds where a reversionary interest in residential leasehold exists within the property.

- Holiday lets
- Time shares
- Beach huts

28. IN SPECIE TRANSFERS AND CONTRIBUTIONS

**"Change will not come if we wait
for some other person or some other time.
We are the ones we've been waiting for.
We are the change that we seek"**

Barack Obama

'In specie' is a Latin term meaning 'in the actual form'. Transferring an asset 'in specie' means to transfer the ownership of that asset from one person or company or entity to another person or company or entity in its current form, which in essence means without the need to convert the asset to cash.

In a SSAS pension context 'in specie' can come in two forms:

- **'In specie' transfers**: this involves a transfer of assets between two pension schemes.

- **'In specie' contributions**: this involves the transfer of assets from an individual or company to a pension scheme.

'In specie' transfers can take the form of shares and property for instance, as well as funds in certain circumstances.

Generally, there will be no dealing costs, however either, or both of the ceding and receiving schemes could charge for the work involved in the transfer. Assets involved need to be properly valued and assessed for suitability by the receiving scheme.

The transfer of the ownership of the assets from the ceding entity to the SSAS happens by re-registering the assets in the name of the SSAS.

This succeeds in getting the assets transferred into the new pension scheme but does not count as a contribution and therefore there is no tax relief. Neither does it count against the annual allowance.

As the assets are not being bought or sold, there are no dealing costs. However, the SSAS administrator might charge for the work involved in changing the ownership of the asset and there could be two charges - on the way 'out' of the existing scheme and on the way 'into' the new one. There may also be solicitors' legal charges depending on the nature of the asset in question.

An 'in specie' transfer can often occur when a member of a pension scheme has started a new SSAS and wishes to transfer existing assets from their old pension scheme to the new SSAS. Both the existing pension provider and the new SSAS administrator must both approve the transfer of assets from a compliance and administrative perspective.

Shares

The process for transferring shares from one pension to another is fairly straight forward. Firstly, the receiving SSAS must request an 'in specie' transfer of assets from the old pension vehicle, via a specific application form that your SSAS administrator will have. This gives the SSAS administrator permission to approach the old pension administrator to request the transfer.

The old pension administrator will then arrange for the share assets to be re-registered in the name of the new SSAS scheme. The process should take somewhere between 3-8 weeks on average.

Commercial Property

The transfer of commercial property commences in a similar way to shares whereby the SSAS Trustee must make a formal transfer request via an application form to the SSAS administrator to facilitate the transfer.

Commercial property is a fairly complex asset class and a property solicitor will need to be formally engaged to change the title of the property and document and register the transfer of ownership with Land Registry. The solicitor will ensure that the receiving SSAS pension will have the due diligence covered, including all conveyancing searches and checks in an identical way as they would if they were purchasing the property. This will ensure that the correct bank grade due diligence process is undertaken, ensuring that the asset is valued correctly, has no flaws in the title, any leases are structured correctly and that no concerns are prevalent in the property.

The commercial property transaction process can take typically 4-12 weeks to complete, depending on the complexity of the asset.

The transfer of an asset to a SSAS as an 'in specie' contribution is usually subject to Stamp Duty Land Tax (SDLT) because although the transfer is for nil consideration, it is a transfer of value all the same. Any Stamp Duty Land Tax payable will be calculated on the open market value of the asset, on the date of the transfer, as verified by an independent specialist valuation. For commercial property this will require an independent valuation from a qualified Royal Institute of Chartered Surveyors (RICS) valuer, normally through a what is known as a Red Book valuation.

Capital Gains Tax may be payable by the transferor depending on its structure and the history of the original purchase. This could be from a company, partnership or individual making the contribution.

Some other additional considerations are important in transferring a commercial property asset into a SSAS, including:

- Joint or multiple ownership of the asset

- Who is the beneficiary of the asset in the event of death?

- Capital gains tax may be payable if there is any increase in property value on disposal.

- VAT and Stamp Duty Land Tax (SDLT) tax issues must be carefully considered

- Annual allowances

29. CORE SKILLS OF A SSAS TRUSTEE

**"Before we acquire great power
we must acquire wisdom to use it well"**

Ralph Waldo Emerson

We have mentioned on numerous occasions within this book the deep sense of accountability and responsibility that a Trustee takes on board when becoming a SSAS Trustee. We are taking ownership of our future pension fund that will need to be managed in such a way that we are able to provide for ourselves and our family as we enter retirement age. The government have more than a passing interest in us being fit, appropriately qualified and equipped to carry out our duties, as in the worst-case scenario of our pension funds being depleted, we would become a burden on the state, which the state wishes to clearly avoid.

As a consequence, SSAS Trustees are subject to requirements imposed by the various Pensions Acts. In addition, HMRC treats Trustees as 'scheme administrators' although this is a function that can be outsourced by the Trustee to a specialist in this area, which in my experience, many choose to do.

Some of the duties of a Trustee/scheme administrator include:

- Registering with The Pensions Regulator and providing a regular scheme return.
- Registering the pension scheme with HMRC.
- Operating tax relief on contributions under the relief at source system.
- Reporting events relating to the scheme and the scheme administrator to HMRC.
- Making returns of information to HMRC.
- Providing information to scheme members and others, regarding the Lifetime Allowance, benefits and transfers.
- Paying certain tax charges.

What is a Trustee?

A Trustee is a person or company acting separately from the employer, who holds assets in the Trust for the beneficiaries of the scheme. Trustees are responsible for ensuring that the pension scheme is run properly, and that members' benefits are secure.

Trustee knowledge and understanding

The law requires that Trustees have knowledge and understanding of the law relating to pensions and Trusts, as well as the principles relating to the funding of pension schemes and the investment of Trust's assets. The law also requires the Trustee to be familiar with certain scheme documents, including the Trust Deed and Rules. You should also familiarise oneself with your statement of investment principles.

The Pensions Regulator's code of practice explains what Trustees need to do in order to comply with the law. For instance, new Trustees must acquire the appropriate knowledge and understanding within six months of being appointed, prompting the immediate question of where that information might come from. This was one of the drivers for writing this book, to help create a roadmap of conscious steps that are required to become a responsible and knowledgeable Trustee.

In becoming a Trustee of a SSAS pension scheme, you are choosing to take on an extremely important role.

As a Trustee, you are responsible for the proper running of the scheme, ranging from the collection of contributions to the investment of assets and payment of benefits. Your fellow Trustees share this responsibility with you and also look to you to play your part in making sure that the scheme is well run and that the benefits are secure.

Who can be a Trustee?

Generally, anyone aged 18 years and over and legally capable of holding property is eligible to be a Trustee. There are some exceptions, which are described below.

A person is disqualified from being a Trustee if:

- They are convicted of an offence involving dishonesty or deception.

- They are an undischarged bankrupt or have entered into certain other voluntary agreements with creditors.

- They have been disqualified from acting as a company director.

- They have a property in Scotland which is covered by a Sequestration Order.

- The person is a company and any director of the company has been disqualified from being a Trustee.

- The person is a Scottish partnership and any of the partners has been disqualified from being a Trustee

Codes of practice

The Pensions Regulator has to issue codes of practice about certain requirements of the Pensions Act 2004 and may issue other codes if it wishes. The codes contain practical guidance on how to comply with the requirements in question and also sets out the standards The Pensions Regulator expects.

A code of practice is not a statement of law - you do not have to follow it.

You can choose to do things differently as long as you can demonstrate that your alternative meets the legal requirements. If a court or tribunal is deciding whether a particular requirement has been met, they will take the code of practice into account.

The Trustees' duties and powers

Many of your duties as a Trustee arise from Trust Law (refer to earlier chapter in this book). These are your 'fiduciary' duties. Your powers derive from the Trust Deed and Rules of the scheme.

This section of the guidance describes the main fiduciary duties and outlines the types of power available to you which includes acting:

- In line with the Trust Deed and Rules

- In the best interests of the scheme beneficiaries

- Impartially
- Responsibly and honestly
- Prudently

These are fundamental for the proper execution of your SSAS Trustee responsibilities so let us take each of these in turn and examine a little more deeply.

Acting in line with the Trust Deed and Rules: The Trust Deed and Rules set out the Trustees' powers and the procedures Trustees must follow. As a Trustee, you must act in line with the terms of the Trust Deed and Rules.

The Trust Deed is a legal document that sets up and governs the scheme.

The scheme Rules set out more detailed conditions on how the scheme operates and would include reference to your statement of investment principles for example.

These are important documents, and Trustees must be familiar with them and with other documents governing the scheme.

Acting in the best interests of the scheme beneficiaries: As a Trustee you must always act in the best interests of the scheme beneficiaries who is defined as anyone who is entitled to a benefit from the scheme, now or in the future.

Beneficiaries can include:

- Active members – employees who are building up benefits in the scheme.
- Pensioner members – people who are receiving a pension from the scheme.
- Deferred members – people who have left the scheme but who still have benefits in it.
- Prospective members – people who may be entitled to join the scheme at a future date.
- Widows and widowers of members.

- Dependants of members – for example, their children or other relatives who financially depend on them.

- Former husbands and wives of members who have been granted pension credits within the scheme.

Acting impartially: You must consider the interests of all beneficiary members covered by the Trust Deed and Rules and act impartially

As a Trustee you must strike a balance between acting in the interests of all the members as a collective, as well as understand the wants, needs and desires of each individual member. The more Trustees there are in a SSAS scheme, the more difficult this can be given the diversity of background, differing objectives and personalities that may be involved.

Acting responsibly and honestly: This duty will touch on many aspects of your work as a Trustee.

When you are acting as a Trustee your duties are to the scheme. Regardless of any other position you may hold, your duty must not be to any group or individual that you are connected with, such as the sponsoring employer.

An example might be the cash flow needs of the sponsoring employer. This is a separate issue and must not influence you while carrying out your Trustee role. That does not to mean the needs of one cannot be considered by the other and vice versa, however this will need to be done in a responsible manner.

The honesty and integrity between Trustees probably rank as one of the higher factors which will dictate the tempo, growth, enjoyment and longevity of your SSAS, as without it there will be significant impairment on these.

Acting prudently: The duty to act prudently means you must act in the way that a prudent person would in their own affairs.

Prudent is defined as "a way that shows care and thought for the future" - you must use any skills and expertise you have at your disposal to consider and undertake your duties in this manner.

This duty is particularly relevant to selecting and dealing with the scheme's investments and should be referenced in the statement of investment principles.

Reaching decisions

As Trustees you will take the responsibility together for your decision making. Each decision will be made in agreement with all Trustees. Your statement of investment principles will be your reference document on what you will invest in and the considerations, ultimate decision making and approval process you go through.

As any organisation would, it is reasonable that you take professional advice on any matters which you do not understand and on technical issues which may affect any investment. This will be part of your due diligence process and will not just be when you decide on making an investment, but also your regular review of existing investments. From time to time you may have to review the SSAS's position in certain investments and reduce, increase or possibly exit from the investment. Each of these decisions requires a diligent approach with any supporting information for Trustees to consider before agreeing on their decision.

A recent example in our SSAS was engaging a Tax Specialist for a commercial property we were acquiring, to ensure that we had VAT registration, VAT considerations and Stamp Duty Land Tax properly considered, ensuring no surprises later during the investment's lifespan.

Personal profit

You must not make any personal profit at the expense of the fund. The Pensions Act 1995 makes it clear that you must keep your personal circumstances separate from your Trustee obligations. As a Trustee and individual, and possibly a company director for example, you must ensure that you wear 'different hats' when operating each entity and making decisions. This can be a difficult concept for new directors or Trustees to get their heads around, however it is important that you do as HMRC are very clear on the rules and any contravention will be met with stiff penalties.

The Trustees' powers

The Trust Deed and Rules give the Trustees powers which will differ from scheme to scheme, however will include all the powers and rights, privileges and discretions they require for the day to day operations of the SSAS. This will enable them to perform all duties required of them by the law.

The Trust Deed would typically include these powers:

- Trustees may delegate any powers and duties to another body.
- Trustees may operate a bank account.
- Decide the investment strategy and invest the scheme's assets.
- Amend the Rules of the scheme.
- Wind up a scheme.

Your Liability

It is important that the Trustees follow the Rules of the scheme. These Rules are set within boundaries defined by:

- The Pension Act
- HMRC
- SSAS Deed of Trust
- SSAS scheme Rules
- Statement of investment principles
- Any other systems you have agreed upon

You must follow these requirements taking advice from any advisers before making decisions about changing circumstances and more complicated issues.

If something goes wrong, Trustees may be personally liable for any loss caused to the scheme as a result of a breach of Trust.

Even if you stop being a Trustee, you are still liable for the decisions you took when you were a Trustee.

What is a breach of trust?

A breach of trust can happen when:

- You carry out an act as a Trustee which you are not authorised to do under the Trust Deed and Rules.

- You fail to do something which you should have done under the Trust Deed and Rules.

- You do not perform one or more of the duties that you have under Trust Law or Pensions Law or do not perform them with sufficient care.

The breach of trust may be unintentional (for example, because of an administrative error), or it may be caused by negligence or through fraudulent and dishonest behaviour.

Joint and several liability

You and your fellow Trustees have 'joint and several liability'. This means you can be held responsible for a breach of trust committed by another Trustee. That is why clear communication and regular Trustee meetings are important to keep abreast of developments of the scheme.

This chapter has been very clear on the detailed responsibilities and skills that you must acquire as you become a SSAS and the importance of mastering them. For most Trustees, there is incredible empowerment by engaging a specialist in this field, such as a SSAS administrator who will help, support, advise and undertake on your behalf to help provide the assurance framework you will require.

I want to highlight some of the equally important skills that you will require in order to make sure your SSAS journey is an enjoyable, engaging and rewarding experience. Many of these will fall into what some may consider as 'life skills. Think of all the social skills, teamwork, leadership and many other skills that you have gained through all your collective experiences in life. These are incredibly valuable.

I have mentored people for nearly 20 years now and a common point that often arises is where people do not recognise the skills and experience that they actually have. They are looking towards the horizon and missing what is at their feet!

An example of this might be someone being concerned that they do not know how to be a Trustee, yet they have previously been a director of a limited company. The knowledge, traits and skills are incredibly similar - this is a huge advantage and will be incredibly helpful in fine tuning that knowledge with the specifics of Trusteeship.

Communication

In my experience whether in business, personal or Trusteeship, the power of communication cannot be underestimated. To truly understand its importance, we should reflect for a moment on the reasons why you decided on establishing a SSAS and who with.

For many it would have been a deeply personal decision, not taken lightly, and undertaken in conjunction with others well known to them. Whether you know your fellow SSAS Trustees well or not, there must be a strong vein of mutual respect and regular, informative and transparent communication will sit at the heart of trust. Without any of these, doubt, distrust, uncertainty, blame and tension will very rapidly seep into the Trustee's relationships. Once this has started to happen it can create significant challenges and can be hard to repair, hence the need to recognise this from the outset.

Mutual respect

Mutual respect will mean different things to different people, however it is crucial that you show respect to your fellow Trustees. This is an exciting journey if performed well. However, relationships will deteriorate quickly if lack of respect, taking each other for granted and not following pre-agreed rules start to happen.

Mutual respect means going the extra mile for each other, putting your best foot forward every time, ensuring performance is also of the highest grade and respecting and protecting the reputation of each of the team, as though it were your own.

Quite often it is the small things that, if done well, can cement relationships and vice versa -the little things that can start to get on people's nerves and quickly escalate. An example could simply be filing of information where it can be quickly and transparently viewed and accessed.

Understanding your fellow Trustees

You decided to establish a SSAS with your fellow Trustees as a long-term strategy, hence you will have strong and productive relationships with your fellow Trustees for many years. Take the time to get to know each other well, understand 'what great looks like' to each other, how you like to operate on a day-to-day basis and how you each gather and assess information. You may find that some of your Trustees are highly analytical and must see the information in a spreadsheet in order to make a decision, whilst others lead more with the concept and emotion and prefer to leave detail to others. As Trustees you must not shy away from this - this is life and we all have different personalities and skills to bring to the table. This should be embraced, recognised and understood and mutually respected. Where there are gaps in confidence, knowledge, information, work together to discuss this and support the overall team in filling those gaps.

The journey together as Trustees is an exciting one which should be embraced, respected and enjoyed. Your fellow Trustees may well be family, friends and trusted associates where great life time bonds can be formed, if undertaken correctly. This is one of the many joys of operating a SSAS – embrace it and immerse yourself with your fellow Trustees. It can be life changing.

30. EARN & LEARN

**"Education is the most powerful weapon
which you can use to change the world"**

Nelson Mandela

For Trustees who are driven to understand and learn the differing strategies that are available, there can be a number of opportunities for collaboration providing a win:win with other parties. This can include an Earn and Learn approach which we use frequently

A great way to start is to consider what skills and assets you have and where you feel you can improve - and use one to fill the other. Let me explain further.

List the areas that you have something that may be of value to others, which may include:

- Funds to invest
- Unencumbered property (i.e. no mortgage and that therefore has a first charge at Land Registry available)
- Time
- Skills that are valuable
- Connections to others

Then list the areas which you may feel the need to strengthen, which may include:

- Knowledge
- Systems
- Investment opportunities
- Education
- Confidence
- Track record

If you can find the overlap where someone has a strength in an area you require and you have something that they need to enable their growth, then there is a great opportunity to provide a win:win for both parties.

The most frequent that I find is an 'Earn and Learn' approach.

I have personally mentored many people over the last 20 years in business, personal development and property development including being a non-executive director since 2008, among other areas. I find mentoring an incredibly fulfilling and mutually rewarding aspect of life.

Trustees may like support and counsel on their commercial development and/or their business strategy, as well as their SSAS journey. They may need guidance on how they can understand more about the opportunities, reality and approach required and what can be achieved in a compliant, assured yet inspirational way that gets them closer to achieving their goals.

Our property development company specialise in commercial to residential conversions and have developments where private capital is funded directly from a number of SSAS Trustees investing their funds on a mutually rewarding 'Earn and Learn' basis.

During the course of the development the SSAS investors gain access to me and the directors of the development business. They visit and understand the processes by which we operate commercial to residential conversion developments, how we achieve the high calibre results, the risk management systems in place and the inner workings of a complex business that thrives on bank grade due diligence and assured outcomes.

An example of Earn and Learn for example might be a Trustee who has a £300,000 fund value and is passionate about learning about commercial property. They could use the loan facility available to them to loan say £100,000 to a developer on a prudent, commercial and secure basis and in return receive a transparent and fulfilling learning experience.

If you are interested in exploring this option with me further, then please email me at mark.stokes@equaSSAS.co.uk.

ROI[4]

Collaboration sits right at the heart of everything we do and the SSAS Alliance is a great example where thousands of like-minded investors regularly connect, discuss, engage and co-invest.

An area which has struck a consistent cord with so many Trustees over the years is the ROI4 model which we have put into practice in collaboration with Kevin Whelan of Wealth Builders.

Together we believe that there are four levels of Return that should exist for any Earn and Learn strategy, all of which simultaneously compounding very effectively, blossoming in many different directions and creating exciting exponential potential. The four levels include:

1. Return OF Investment: ensure the capital sum is secure and will be returned at the end of the term.

2. Return ON Investment: enabling an equitable return on the investment.

3. Return on Interaction: connecting people and process

4. Return on Intellect: providing a transparent and beneficial learning experience for the investor.

ROI⁴

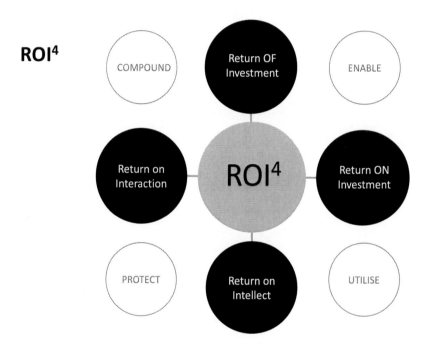

Interwoven through each of these four levels of return is the ability for you to enable, utilise, protect and compound your knowledge and your SSAS asset valuation.

Whether you are a SSAS Trustee or a private investor via other means, these fundamentals invariable tick a number of boxes for many and provide an extremely engaging and trustworthy relationship based on:

- Creating shared value
- Exchanging shared value
- Sustainability
- Long term relationships
- A win:win for both parties

31. YOUR TEAM

**"If you think it is expensive to hire a professional
to do the job, wait until you hire an amateur"**

Red Adair

Independent Financial Advisor

Independent Financial Advisers (IFA) are professionals who offer independent advice on financial matters to their clients and recommend suitable financial products from the market.

Typically, an Independent Financial Adviser will conduct a detailed survey of a client's financial position, preferences and objectives; this is sometimes known as a 'fact find'. The adviser will then recommend appropriate action to meet the client's objectives and, if necessary, recommend a suitable financial product to match the client's needs.

Individuals and businesses consult IFAs on many matters including investment, retirement planning, insurance, protection and mortgages (or other loans). IFA's also advise on some tax and legal matters. Some IFA's many not be aware of SSAS pensions in any detail - hence do your research and ensure you secure the advice of an IFA who truly does understand all the viable options available to you.

To offer financial advice, an individual must represent or be an appointed representative of a firm registered with the Financial Conduct Authority (FCA).

SSAS Administrator

The SSAS administrator is the entity who runs the pension scheme. As well as this general duty, the SSAS administrator has particular obligations to provide information to HMRC, the pension scheme member and The Pensions Regulator.

The SSAS administrator is the party responsible for notifying, within the deadline, any reportable events including the annual HMRC pension scheme return and accounting for any tax due. They are the party who will provide the overwatch and administration of the day-to-day operations of the Trust on behalf of the Trustees. This is the responsibility of the Trustees, who in most cases will decide to outsource this function to a specialist SSAS administration organisation.

Throughout this book we refer to the generic term 'SSAS administrator', however there are four types of roles which you may consider in driving your SSAS Trust, as follows:

Member Trustees: These have the ultimate responsibility to The Pension Regulator and HMRC for the overall SSAS compliance with pension law.

Scheme Administrator: This role oversees the scheme and its assets in a formal engagement by the Trustees to assist them in complying with pensions law. The Scheme Administrator is also responsible for completing and submitting returns to HMRC. Often the scheme administrator will be a sole signatory bank account from which all financial transactions are made. This enables the Member Trustees to delegate the administration of transactions and can help ensure that valuable pension assets remain protected from breaching HMRC rules.

Professional Trustee: or 'Independent Trustee' is appointed by the Trustees to support them in complying with pensions Law. A Professional Trustee will be a co-signatory on scheme assets and can act to prevent certain investments and actions if they will cause harm or high levels of risk to the SSAS or give rise to HMRC charges.

Scheme Practitioner: Whilst a scheme must appoint a Scheme Administrator, a Scheme Practitioner is not a formal role but supports the Scheme Administrator and the member Trustees in complying with pension law.

Should you engage with an external scheme administrator you will be asked to sign an Administration Service Agreement (ASA) which will be your contract between all parties.

The scheme administrator's role is to advise the Trustees on the ever-changing administration and tax rules set out by HM Revenue & Customs. As HMRC does not offer any ongoing guidance or support to your SSAS directly, it is strongly advisable to have an experienced scheme administrator in place. The penalties levied by HMRC for any unauthorised payments by your scheme can be severe.

The scheme administrator may be a member of a recognised industry body such as AMPS (Association of Member-Directed Pension Schemes) or possibly SSAS Alliance. AMPS has more than 150 member firms representing many parts of the member-directed pensions industry, including SSAS administrators.

Your scheme administrator will provide you with all administration and technical advice relating to your SSAS, as well as give you all of the required scheme documentation. They will also maintain scheme records in accordance with the Information Commissioner Office data protection requirements, including GDPR.

Your scheme administrator will also complete all required HMRC reports, assist Trustees regarding the purchase and sale of scheme assets, and provide any calculations for members' benefit payments.

A scheme practitioner is also invaluable in the event of a dispute between members and would be able to mediate without having to involve regulatory bodies or solicitors.

Running a SSAS is not an easy task; HMRC rules are very stringent and it is not usually advisable for Trustees to act as administrators, or not until they have become very experienced, although there are exceptions.

What does independence mean to you?

This might be a question you consider between the Trustees as you decide who to select as your SSAS administrator.

Some SSAS administrators have very specific investment opportunities or associated funds that they may overtly open up to you for investment. You will need to decide how comfortable you see this service. Do you see it as a benefit? Is it an opportunity? Does it sit with the objectives of your statement of investment principles? Is it being sold to us? Does it make economic sense, compared to the other opportunities you are considering? Will it restrict our investment strategy?

Most SSAS administrators play an entirely independent role and only have a financial interest in terms of fees for a schedule of services provided.

Some of the functions that are undertaken by the scheme administrator include:

- Registering the pension scheme with HM Revenue & Customs (HMRC).

- Setting up a bank account.

- Operating tax relief on contributions under the relief at source system.

- Reporting events relating to the scheme and the scheme administrator to HMRC.

- Making annual returns of information to HMRC and The Pension Regulator.

- Register the pension scheme with The Pensions Regulator.

- Reporting events relating to the scheme and the scheme administrator to The Pensions Regulator.

- Providing information to scheme members regarding the Lifetime Allowance, benefits and transfers.

- Pension scheme documentation to address changes in legislation.

- A scheme takeover service where required.

- Pre-investment review service to assess proposed investments.

- Annual member statements.

- Calculation and periodic review of pension benefits.

- Trustee meetings as required.

- Pension Payroll Services.

For many, the path most trodden is to engage with a SSAS administrator who will be a company. As any company can have challenges along the way, let us touch on your protection should your SSAS Administrator go out of business, for whatever reason. If this happens, your pension assets will be safe, and the following process would happen:

- All funds are held in your Trust and do not form part of any other legal entities balance sheet so cannot be accessed by creditors.

- You have FSCS protection for regulated investments such as the pooled Trustee bank account which protects you where the bank fails.

- A receiver would be appointed to handle transfer of any administrator's business activities to other providers.

- The receiver is likely to maintain staff to ensure this process operates smoothly.

Whilst the likelihood of this happening is probably very low of course, any organisation can encounter issues hence it is sensible and pragmatic to ensure you engage with a well-known and well-structured company, with a substantial track record, that can offer the services you require. Whilst there would be some inconvenience for sure, the process outlined above would broadly ensure there is no disadvantage to you other than some possible administrative delays while your pension scheme is moved.

Solicitor

A solicitor may be required for numerous elements of SSAS activity. You may choose to take advice in areas such as independent legal advice as a Trustee, to review any contracts, to oversee investor loan, and the SSAS may appoint a solicitor to undertake transaction work such as property transactions.

Should a lender be appointed to provide financial leverage, they may specifically require personal guarantees from the individual Trustees. Should this be the case you will need to ask a suitably qualified solicitor to take advice and they will have to certify that you signed the personal guarantees in the certified knowledge and understanding of what you were signing - and not under duress.

Accountant

Depending on the complexity of your SSAS operations, you may choose to appoint an accountant to manage the process of your records and filings.

Many SSAS administrators undertake this process as a matter of course, as part of the engagement process, and you should check thoroughly if the services you are contracting covers these areas.

If engaging a separate accountant due to the diversity, quantum and specialism of your SSAS investments, then interview and research the potential accountant's expertise, specifically in the area of SSAS pension schemes, as there are crucial requirements which will need to be adhered to.

As the old saying goes: 'you wouldn't want an eye surgeon operating on your heart!'.

Many Trustees may choose to provide additional responsibility to their existing accountant who is familiar with their overall personal economy, including personal tax returns and any company account management. This can simplify the process significantly.

Tax advisor

As Trustees we should not leave anything to chance. A SSAS is a highly tax efficient vehicle at one end of the spectrum and a vehicle that, if operated ineffectively, can induce significant penalties and liabilities for the uneducated and naive.

You have purchased this book so should not fall into either of those later categories and should be well on your way to advancing your continuous professional development.

A great tax advisor is always recommended, and this may be an appointment you make in conjunction with your accountants' role or separately. You may also choose to combine this role (albeit through a separate engagement contract) with other tax advise that you seek for your other wealth interests.

Bank

A bank account is an important part of establishing your SSAS and enabling your pension funds to be transferred into.

Your governance process will need to structure how you finalise your bank mandate in terms of the protocol of who can operate the bank account, how payments are made and maintain audit and control at all stages.

Government are increasingly tightening the checks that banks need to make in order to approve the opening of a bank account. These checks fall under the Anti Money Laundering (AML) checks covering areas such as 'Know Your Client' (KYC) due diligence.

If you have decided to engage a SSAS administrator, then this is something that they frequently deal with.

Insurance

Insurance is a specialist area and may be a requirement to one degree or another, based on the agreed operations of your SSAS. You may have to consider other parties' requirements as well. For example, if you are bringing in leverage in the form of senior debt funding from a bank, possibly for a commercial property acquisition, they will make insurance a condition precedent in the funding documents which must be satisfied prior to the loan/ mortgage being drawn down.

A detailed understanding of your insurance strategy and structure is where an insurance broker will serve your business well as a key part of your professional team.

Some of the levels of insurance that you will need to consider for your business may include:

- Business insurance

- Buildings and contents insurance

- Joint names policy

- Contractors all-risk
- Professional indemnity
- Key man insurance
- Public liability
- Employers' liability

There are many variant themes of insurance and your specific strategy must be discussed openly with your insurance broker to ensure you have the correct cover required.

One of the more complex areas for insurance is property and if this is part of your SSAS investment strategy, you will need to be clear on what type of investment you are considering.

As an example, if you are acquiring a retail premises with a single, full repair and insure (FRI) lease in place with a commercial tenant that would require one set of insurance policies. The insurance considerations would be very different if purchasing a commercial property and then developing through partial demolition, rebuilding or extension.

You must always insure the property you are purchasing at the point of exchange of contracts. At exchange, you're legally obliged to purchase the building at a period of time in the future (stated in the exchange contract).

Should that building burn down between the point which you have exchanged and your specific completion date, you will still have to complete on the purchase. Therefore, it is vital that full insurance is in place at the point of exchange.

Engagement of your professional team and also your main contractor will be very important in the assurance process of which insurance covers a critical layer of diligence. Your senior debt funder, if you have one, will also be highly observant and will want to understand your insurance structure and the levels of which public liability, professional indemnity and employers' liability cover are engaged.

Do bear this in mind in your due diligence and pre-qualification of your professional team and main contractor and make the insurance requirements a condition of contract.

Other specialist services

Depending on your investment strategy you may require different skills to focus on risk management and execution of a certain investment or asset class. These may include:

- **Commercial property agent**: required during commercial property transactions particularly the sale process.
- **Commercial property solicitor**: required to conduct all searches and the transaction process of the purchase of a property and its filing at Land Registry.
- **Project Manager**: required to oversee property development, as an example.
- **Commercial Manager**: usually employed to manage property development contracts and cost control. This can often be combined with the duties of the project manager.
- **Surveyors**: these can be many and varied and are typically involved in property purchases. They may include party wall surveyors, structural surveyors, environmental engineers, contamination specialists, building surveyors, refurbishment and demolition surveyors etc.
- **Planning Consultant**: required should you look to enhance, or change, the property through development or for planning gain purposes.
- **Design team**: required for property development including architect, building services, structural and environmental etc.
- **RICS Valuer**: this is the surveyor that will undertake the RICS Red Book Valuation required by the SSAS, bank lenders and possibly investors.
- **VAT specialist**
- **Stockbroker**
- **Fund Manager**

32.CASE STUDY – SSAS ACQUISITION AND LEASE BACK

"Real estate cannot be lost or stolen, nor can it be carried away. Purchased with common sense, paid for in full, and managed with reasonable care, it is about the safest investment in the world"

Franklin D. Roosevelt

The following is a scenario showing a SSAS pension in practice examining a sale and leaseback of commercial land and property.

Angela and Mike have been married for 30 years and they have both made savings to pensions over the years:

- Angela has a £90,000 personal pension
- Mike has a £130,000 personal pension

They have their own business owned 50:50, which is a limited company.

The company is expected to make a profit of £200,000 before their year-end and it currently holds surplus cash reserves of £100,000.

Angela and Mike are interested in purchasing land next to their business premises for £300,000 and have been considering using their £100,000 cash reserves and a bank loan but want to keep the interest payments to a minimum.

The approach they have decided upon is to establish a SSAS with the business as the sponsoring employer, with Angela and Mike as members. They will then transfer their existing pension funds of £220,000 into the SSAS.

The business will then make an employer pension contribution to the SSAS of £40k each for both Angela and Mike, as they have salaries at that level. Their SSAS will then be valued at £300,000. The business benefit is not lost on Angela or Mike in that the pension contribution made by the business will have the potential of reducing the corporate tax payable on the current year's profits.

Angela and Mike now plan to use the SSAS to purchase the land without having to raise any borrowing via a bank, thus reducing the cost of capital significantly. The SSAS will own the land with Angela and Mike as 50:50 joint owners of the SSAS.

They then plan to lease the land back to the business with the rent payable by the business being a cost and therefore will effectively further reduce corporation tax payable. The incoming rent received by the SSAS pension will compound in the SSAS for years to come and may well be reinvested into future investment opportunities to furthermore enhance the compounded growth.

Overall the beauty of this model is that all the funds, income and interest remain in the personal economy of Angela and Mike - it is their own circular wealth economy!

33. SSAS TAKEOVER - CHANGING YOUR SSAS ADMINISTRATOR

"All the knowledge I possess everyone else can acquire, but my heart is all my own"

Johann Wolfgang von Goethe

As in any professional services relationship, it may be the relationship between you and your SSAS administrator has run its course and you wish to transfer to a different organisation.

There may be many reasons for this including:

- Unsatisfied with performance
- Different level of skills required
- You decide you wish to self-manage your SSAS
- You decide you do not wish to self-manage any longer
- SSAS Administrator has a different policy and interpretation to you
- You wish to join another SSAS
- You would like more flexibility in your investment strategy
- SSAS Administrator gets into financial difficulties

Because SSAS's are set up as separate standalone trusts with members also being Trustees, should a SSAS administrator experience financial or other difficulties, the Trustees could simply replace them with another administrator to take over the day to day running of the scheme.

If this is the case, then Trustees can elect to move the SSAS administrator role via a process called Takeover.

This would normally be carried out as follows:

- The new SSAS administrator sends the Trustees a SSAS takeover questionnaire and a draft letter from the Trustees to the current service provider to inform them that they are to be replaced, for completion and return.
- The new SSAS administrator provides an estimate of the likely costs of the takeover and ongoing annual charges.
- The new SSSAS administrator sends the Trustees' letter to the current service provider, together with a letter asking for copies of the SSAS documents (e.g. Trust Deeds and Rules,

Trustee resolutions, HMRC registered status and accounts) and information about members, investments and bank accounts etc.

- The new SSAS administrator provides Deeds, as necessary, to

    a. Appoint Trustee company

    b. Remove any existing professional Trustee

    c. Replace the existing Trust Deed and Rules with the new SSAS administrators set, which places the power of amendment, the power of appointment and removal of Trustees in the hands of the Trustees.

- The new SSAS administrator will re-register all investments, including bank accounts, so they are a co-holder with the other Trustees. This might also include the new SSAS administrator being a mandatory signatory on each bank account.

- The new SSAS administrator arranges for their inclusion to the Trustees' VAT registration.

- The new SSAS administrator arranges for the appropriate changes to be made to the SSAS's online records with HMRC, The Pensions Regulator and the Information Commissioner's Office.

- The new SSAS administrator then advises formally all other relevant parties of their appointment.

- The new SSAS administrator then provides ongoing professional administration services.

You will be required to complete a SSAS takeover questionnaire which would typically include:

- Reasons for the proposed change

- Target date for Takeover

- Name and details of existing SSAS administrator

- Role of current Professional Trustee/practitioner:

  Co-Trustee

  SSAS administrator

  Joint signatory

  Practitioner only
- Scheme year end accounts
- Trustees bank account and details
- VAT registration details and who completes the returns
- Member details:

  Name

  Address

  Contact details

  Date of birth

  National Insurance number

  Member status

  Is pension income being drawn

  Next formal review date

  Break down of allocation of funds between members
- Proof of ID and address
- Investment details
- Copy of latest scheme accounts
- Has the pension scheme return been completed and sent to HMRC?
- Details of current level of fees
- Any specific request on duties required and level of service
- Any issues requiring attention

Your due diligence is hugely important in selecting the right SSAS administrator for you and your requirements

I have seen instances where people have got so bogged down in trying to make the decision as to which SSAS administrator to go for that they have procrastinated and then spend several years, in some cases, not making any decision at all. This has arguably lost them significant value, learning and progress.

The takeover process is straight forward in principle, however the complexity will depend on the assets that you hold within your SSAS. Take these two examples of a SSAS that has a valuation of £455,000:

Example 1:
You have a SSAS with a current valuation of £455,000 with an asset distribution as follows:

- £305,000   Cash
- £150,000   Loan back to sponsoring company

This process will be very straight forward, given the availability of the right information and the whole process will probably take between 4-8 weeks.

Example 2:
You have a SSAS with a current valuation of £455,000 with an asset distribution as follows:

- £70,000   Cash
- £40,000   Share portfolio
- £50,000   Loan A to an unconnected third party
- £15,000   Loan B to an unconnected third party
- £100,000   Loan back to sponsoring company
- £180,000   Commercial property owned with 20% bank leverage

The greater complexity of the example 2 strategy will take a little longer to conclude and may result in a higher fee structure to undertake the process. It will be down to your assessment in taking a long-term view of cost 'v' benefit of doing this and the fundamental reasons why you are considering a take-over in the first place.

A key message I want you to take away from this section is that you are NOT married for life, and beyond, to your SSAS administrator and the Takeover process should be viewed as similar to that of changing your accountant in business life. It is not ideal, can cause a bit of extra work, cost, time and inconvenience but it will not be fatal and will be completed in only a few months - and you can then get on with managing your SSAS with a new administrator.

So, do not procrastinate in making a decision on your SSAS administrator. Once you are sure the SSAS route is for you, and you're comfortable with the accountability that it requires, do your due diligence on potential SSAS administrators. When you then make a decision, you can do it fully committed, knowing that, should circumstances change, you can make informed decisions to protect your interests at that time.

34. TAKING BENEFITS

**"Every adversity, every failure,
every heartache carries with it the seed
of an equal or greater benefit"**

Napoleon Hill

The words 'pension' and 'retirement' are frequently used in concert with each other. However, it is not always necessary to retire in the normal sense of the word, to start reaping the rewards. You could still be working, you could still own your business, however part of your overall income comes from your pension pot – it's all about choice and flexibility.

Many of us love what we do and the energy and mental stimulation of working with like-minded people, creating massive shared value and supporting others through education and collaboration.

We may choose to reduce our time in certain aspects and hand over the day-to-day reigns of management. However, the knowledge, counsel and mentoring that we have worked a lifetime in finely honing is immensely valuable and rewarding to the future generation who will often be the custodians of our legacy – it would be a shame to give up this enjoyable part of giving back to others.

A SSAS can take advantage of the governments 2015 flexible drawdown options to offer control and flexibility in the area of Pension Contributions and Investments.

A SSAS is an extremely flexible solution for retirement income drawdown and also business exit options - at the age of 55, you can commence drawdown from your pension fund.

You can draw the first 25% of your pension fund tax free, due to the 2015 changes in pension legislation - and then you can take the remainder of the cash as you wish and only pay marginal rate tax, as and when you draw it.

Marginal rate means the amount you drawdown will attract PAYE as if it were salary.

For example:

- Your Trustee fund holds £320,000 at age 55, the available tax-free lump sum will be £80k.

- You choose to take the other £240,000 at £10,000 per year; you will pay no income tax on that £10,000 if you have no other income.

- If you choose to take the entire fund, you will pay a higher rate of Tax under the PAYE scheme at marginal rates.

Being in control of your own SSAS allows you the flexibility of choices and the ability to adapt to changing circumstances, as inevitably life takes its twists and turns.

Of course, if your SSAS has acquired commercial property then you can still receive rent even when you have retired.

Your retirement options

For most people, the earliest age they can take retirement benefits is 55 – although, as we continue to live longer, this minimum age may increase (see chart in chapter 3).

Broadly, you can take a tax-free lump sum of 25% of the value of your pension and you then have choices to make about what to do with the rest - whether you buy an annuity, whether you draw an income directly from your SSAS or whether you consider transferring the pot to an alternative type of pension.

From April 2015 legislation was changed to give greater pension freedom and so gives more choice to people upon retirement. The new rules mean that it is possible to receive your entire fund as a one-off income payment whereby 25% of the fund would be paid to you, free of tax, but the remainder of the payment would be subject to tax at your marginal rate.

Before you make any decisions, it is important to consult your Independent Financial Adviser as this can be extremely tax inefficient.

As we move into the detail of different scenarios and options of drawdown of funds, we will refer to 'crystallised' and 'uncrystallised' funds. This refers to whether you have taken some benefits from your pension, referred to as crystallised, or if you have not taken benefits then the fund would be referred to as uncrystallised.

What happens when you die?

Never a nice thought but it is the only certainty of life, so we had better understand what happens. In the event of death, the two main scenarios are around the age you were at the time of your passing, as detailed below:

Death before age 75

In the event of a SSAS Trustees' death before the age of 75, and irrespective as to whether retirement benefits have been drawn, the whole of their fund, including life cover up to the Lifetime Allowance, can normally be paid out as a lump sum or as income payments to their nominated beneficiaries, tax free.

The Trustees uncrystallised funds in the SSAS would be tested against the Trustees remaining Lifetime Allowance and any excess will be subject to a Lifetime Allowance tax charge.

Death after age 75

Should a SSAS Trustee die after reaching aged 75, the remaining funds can be paid to beneficiaries as a lump sum or pension income. Pension income can only be paid to individuals. Lump sums, as well as pension income paid to individuals, will be assessed as income for the purposes of tax.

Should lump sums be paid to another party, such as Trusts and companies, these sums would be subject to a special tax charge of 45%.

It may be of interest that in certain circumstances, lump sums to charities can be tax-free.

Once again, tax planning is essential and gaining the counsel and wisdom of an excellent tax advisor as well as an accountant, will pay in the long run.

What happens when my beneficiary dies?

When a SSAS Trustee's nominated beneficiary dies whilst receiving benefits from the fund, benefits can then be paid to their beneficiaries in turn. This can then be repeated as generations pass, until the fund has been exhausted. The tax treatment of the benefits will depend upon the beneficiary's age at death and to whom the benefits are to be paid. This gives the potential for Trustees to pass pension funds down, through the generations, with the funds remaining invested in a highly tax efficient environment.

Should a Trustee die and there are no dependants, or nominated beneficiaries to whom benefits can be paid, the fund can be:

- Returned to the employer less a 35% tax charge.

- Retained by the Trustees to be reallocated to other members.

- Given to a charity, previously nominated by the deceased member, tax-free.

When you die, your pension does not die with you and any remaining funds will be passed to your beneficiaries. The amount and type of benefits depend on how much remains in the fund, at what age you die, and the benefit options chosen.

The remaining Trustees have discretion over who they pay benefits to and will be guided by your wishes, which you will have indicated in an 'expression of wishes' form. It is essential that you not only complete this document clearly but also to review it and update it to ensure that, at any time, it fully represents your wishes. Circumstances can change, disagreements can happen, planned beneficiaries can pass away, people get married or divorced etc. Keeping on top of this will ensure your expressed wishes of your legacy does not become a source of non-clarity or contention after your passing.

Your beneficiaries may choose to take any remaining money as a lump sum. Equally, they may prefer to have a regular income until the fund is depleted.

Importantly, the funds held in your SSAS pension will not form part of your estate, and so will be treated separately for inheritance tax purposes.

Over recent years the approach to pensions would appear to be more balanced and some might say fairer, and more flexible, than has been the case in the past.

More of your fund benefit can be passed to your beneficiaries; you have more choice and you can have more confidence in your investment planning.

When Members are ready to draw their pension, they have a number of options available to them. Drawdown allows clients to retain control of their SSAS pension fund assets while receiving an income from them. Here are the most widely utilised drawdown options and consideration:

Transfer to another provider

You can transfer your benefits to another pension provider or providers. Different pension providers may offer different flexible pension options, including the option to select an annuity, which may be something that appeals to you.

Knowing all the options that are available to you will enable you to plan this well ahead of time.

Flexi-access drawdown pension

This form of drawdown pension allows a SSAS Trustee to draw a pension income from their crystallised funds within the SSAS, with no upper limit other than the value of those funds.

We must be planning carefully ahead and understand the risk reward profile we need. We must bear in mind that this limitation on funds whilst obvious, is sometimes overlooked.

It is perfectly possible, with poor planning, to run out of funds to support yourself in the future. Examples of reason why might include:

- SSAS investments perform poorly

- Trustee draws too much pension

- Trustee lives longer than expected

What a miserable state of affairs if you're living longer than expected, creates pressure, pain and financial hardship!!!

I am sure we all wish to live as long as possible with great health and sufficient wealth to enable us to continue to have a wide array of choices and freedom in life.

The first payment of flexi-access drawdown will mean that the Money Purchase Annual Allowance of £4,000 pa gross currently will then apply to contributions paid by, or for, the Trustee to the SSAS and any other money purchase registered pension schemes they may have.

This form of drawdown allows you to take as much or as little as you want. However, if you use this option your Annual Allowance, which is the amount you can contribute to your pension without incurring tax charges, will reduce once an income payment has been taken. Any lump sums you take are tax free (up to 25%) and the drawdown payments are taxed as income; the rate of tax that applies will depend on the amount of income that you receive from other sources.

Uncrystallised funds pension lump sum

This allows a Member to take a lump sum from their uncrystallised funds within the SSAS, 25% of which is normally tax-free, and the balance is assessable income for tax purposes. The lump sum must be paid in one go. Payment of an uncrystallised fund pension lump sum will mean the Money Purchase Annual Allowance of £4,000 pa gross currently will then apply in relation to contributions by, or for, the Trustee to the SSAS and any other money purchase registered pension schemes they may have.

Lifetime annuity

If a Trustee decides to use their SSAS funds to buy an annuity from an insurance company, the terms of the annuity will normally be determined at that time. They can include features such as annual increases, at a set percentage, or in line with inflation and provision for annuity payments to a spouse or other dependant in the event of the Member's death.

The actual level of annuity a Member can buy will depend on their age, health and annuity rates at that time.

An annuity usually provides a secure and set level of income for the rest of a Member's life. It is not normally possible to cancel an annuity contract or vary its terms. However, if the annuity is a 'flexible annuity', payments can decrease and do not have to continue for life.

A scheme pension is a secured income paid to the Trustee for life. It is worth reiterating that unlike income drawdown, a scheme pension can provide a guaranteed income.

A scheme pension allows the Trustee to receive an income direct from the SSAS. The SSAS provides the Member with a set level of pension in return for their fund. Typically, the level of pension is calculated by your provider and is designed to pay out the fund over the Member's expected lifetime.

A lifetime annuity is purchased from a life assurance company. The annuity must be payable up to the Member's death, or the end of any guarantee period, should the Member die within this period.

The annuity may be level or incorporate annual increases and may also allow for dependants' pensions to be paid after the death of the annuitant.

Short-term annuity

A short-term annuity is purchased from a life assurance company and is payable for a term of no more than five years.

The 2015 government decision to allow those reaching aged 55 to withdraw a tax-free lump sum of 25%, is a great example where knowing the details is incredibly important as pitfalls can exist.

At the time of writing this book in very early 2019, reports are starting to emerge of many people who took advantage of this opportunity possibly now becoming at risk of getting unexpected tax bills. This is possibly occurring after inadvertently prompting a substantial cut in their tax-free pension savings allowance by delving too deep into their pension fund causing an irreversible reduction in their annual pension tax relief allowance from £40,000 to £4,000.

In any strategy it pays to research exactly the implications of any decision and this is a serious case in point as it is possible that many over 55's, who took the tax-free lump sum, may be unaware that their tax relief limits and have an unrecognised tax liability. Worrying times indeed ahead as they firstly recognise that they may have a problem and then start to address what that means - and how they can settle their tax liabilities at a time when they should be enjoying the rewards of their hard endeavours.

Sadly, this is another example of where the bright lights of flashy headlines and their apparent benefits can quickly unravel, if one does not do their due diligence on cause and effect.

If you had paid more than your annual allowance into your pension, these would be subject to tax charges at their top marginal rate on the excess amount.

For example: Stephen is a 58-year-old higher-rate taxpayer who took his 25% tax free lump sum and has now invested it on a long-term basis. This withdrawal of the tax-free lump sum prompted a cut in his annual allowance from £40,000 to £4,000.

Stephen then continued to pay £15,000 per year into his pension without checking the detailed implications. This would mean that Stephen has exceeded his allowable contributions by £11,000 (£15,000 - £4,000) and as a higher rate 40% tax payer, he could well be liable for a £4,400 tax bill.

The reduced allowance was intended to prevent people using the new pension freedoms to recycle money through a pension and effectively receive additional tax relief on those savings. It is now set at £4,000.

So where did the £4,000 limit come from? Any individual who withdraws funds from a pension above a prescribed level can only subsequently put in new savings of up to £4,000 a year without incurring a tax charge. This is substantially below the standard £40,000 limit.

As is always the case in any detailed matter, always take the most appropriate and qualified advice, in this case from your Independent Financial Advisor, to avoid straying into areas of non-compliance or tax charges.

35. WINDING UP A SSAS

"The most important thing is that we are on the right path, and we will not deviate from it, even in the face of strong temptation to choose temporary gains over long-term benefits"

Yemi Osinbajo

There are two main areas to focus on here, namely:

- Winding up a SSAS Trust
- Winding up a sponsoring company to a SSAS Trust

The SSAS may be wound up at any time. Members benefits must be first secured, with any non-allocated funds being paid back to the business, less a 35% tax charge.

Why would a SSAS want to be wound up? As we discussed earlier, there are a number of different types of SSAS such as Solo, Family and Team SSAS. Circumstances can change for Trustees such as the prosperity of the sponsoring company, although the longevity of this organisation does not necessarily have a bearing on the SSAS itself. Further actions would need to be taken regarding a new sponsoring company for instance.

Trustees individual circumstances may alter in terms of appetite, risk, financial objectives, circumstances, relationship, animosity and disagreement or death etc.

The relationship that you currently enjoy with your fellow Trustees may not be replicable with their beneficiaries, should they pass away. They may not understand a SSAS scheme or may have entirely differing values, backgrounds and aspirations for the future.

As we know, SSAS's are a Trust and they are governed and operated in accordance with their Trust Deed and Rules. While a large portion of the rules will be standard and relate to legislation, covering accrual and payments of retirement and death benefits, a wide variety of options exist as to whom the powers to operate the scheme are vested and how the scheme should be treated in the circumstance of the wind up, or sale of the company.

Dealing firstly with a sale or wind up of a company, some SSAS Deeds may specify that in either of these situations the scheme should be wound up, with benefits transferred to alternative individual arrangements.

This will very rarely be desirable because a SSAS will often hold a wide range of assets. However, it is possible to continue to run a

SSAS without a sponsoring company, provided the scheme Rules allow for this.

It should also be borne in mind that HM Revenue & Customs have powers to deregister an occupational pension scheme such as a SSAS, where the sponsoring company has become dormant.

This is an additional tool to help HMRC try to prevent pension scams, but they have stated that it is their intention only to deregister pension schemes 'where there is clear evidence that it is not being used to provide legitimate pension benefits within the tax rules'.

The endearing benefits and features of a SSAS appeal significantly to an entrepreneur due to its substantial benefits to businesses. Entrepreneurs rarely retire completely, often having other companies, which may be able to interact with the SSAS prior to the sale, or wind up, of the original sponsoring company.

If this is the case, it could be possible to substitute the existing sponsoring company with another sponsoring company, subject to adhering to the Trust Rules, and the SSAS then continues as normal. Depending on the scheme Rules, it may only be possible for a new sponsoring company to be approved with the consent of the existing sponsoring company.

An important point to note is that a SSAS can legitimately have more than one sponsoring company.

It would, therefore, be prudent to address this issue before any sale or wind up of the existing sponsoring company takes place – for example, by ensuring that the scheme Rules are amended to permit the adherence even after the existing sponsoring company has been sold or wound up.

It would also be wise to make any other necessary amendments to the scheme Rules so that the existing sponsoring company no longer has any powers, under the scheme Rules, including the power to amend the scheme Rules, the power to appoint and remove Trustees and the power to admit new members to the scheme.

Failure to address these issues, ahead of a sale or wind up of a sponsoring company, might result in the scheme becoming almost impossible to administer or require expensive legal advice and assistance.

36. ENJOYMENT & LIFESTYLE

**"In the end it is not the years in your life,
it is the life in your years"**

Abraham Lincoln

This chapter heading may seem a little warm and fluffy for some, however, I know it has been important to me and I am sure many existing Trustees will relate to this.

If Trusteeship is something you aspire to, I can assure that you will experience many intangible benefits as well as tangible benefits that will remain profoundly important in the overall journey of life.

A unique feature of a SSAS is that no manual, roadmap or structured counsel exists, until this book of course!

Furthermore, nowhere have I ever seen any suggestion that it can be fun and enjoyable. I have certainly not heard that language from many financial advisors that is for sure!

Well it is true – it is fun, liberating and extremely enjoyable.

It is genuinely true and this should be really understood. The feeling of having your own SSAS and having freedom and choice is absolutely liberating, if you choose it to be.

Yes, a SSAS scheme comes with significant responsibility and accountability which we have covered extensively. However, so does running any other legal entity such as a company, charity, partnership etc. We can have fun running those too, so why not allow the running of a SSAS to be massively fun as well!

With a SSAS, fun and enjoyment shouldn't just be a by-product of the act of running the SSAS - it should be a fundamental goal, a reason in itself for operating a SSAS and also something that is shared with possibly your family unit, perfectly aligned with your values and long-term goals.

The inspiration of knowing what a SSAS can achieve and then trail blazing the execution of a clear and articulate plan, enabling your goals and targets to be realised, is truly compelling.

Many of my Trustee friends have incredibly poignant goals often centring on family and wonderfully meaningful life changing targets that are incredibly personal to them.

From personal experience I know the enjoyment that comes from operating a SSAS and some of these that are shared by many include:

- An overall deep sense of satisfaction
- Learning new subject matters
- Growing one's intellect
- Improving one's confidence
- Mastering something you are in full control of
- Meeting like-minded people who share your passion
- Opening up a new circle of friends
- Getting to know new people
- Social gatherings of SSAS Trustees comparing notes, supporting each other such as the SSAS Alliance Business Network.
- Collaboration
- Using a SSAS to enable your own personal economy
- Creating massive shared value
- Satisfaction of making your own investment decisions
- Attending educational and learning events with SSAS Alliance
- Earning whilst learning
- Catalytic in forging long term strategic thinking relating to your own wealth creation

At the time of writing I am in my late forties and rapidly approaching my half century. Over my 30 years in business I have met some incredible people who have now become dear friends through business connections, shared passions and mutual interests. Many of these initial discussions have turned into business relationships and I savour every one of them.

Since becoming a SSAS Trustee I can honestly say that the richness of relationships with new found Trustees has only served to further enrich my life, for which I am filled with gratitude.

Having fun and making new friendships is part of life and amongst SSAS Trustees there is something very precious, a bond that exists based on common values, deep respect, an inquisitive mind and a mutual appreciation of respective positions. This is bonded by a transparency which is not only refreshing, but unprecedented in many walks of life and something that establishes sincere and deep bonds of Trust.

Within the SSAS Alliance we are enabling our members to connect with each other and share truly meaningful experiences of life, as well as supporting each other in areas which many of us find of value.

A few examples of these that are currently being planned within the SSAS Alliance community include:

- SSAS Ski Retreat
- Formula 1 Race day
- Health and well-being events
- Fitness programme
- Super car track days
- Golf competition
- Podcast
- Younger Generation Business Experience taster sessions
- Education
- Regional Business Network
- SSAS Alliance Annual Awards Dinner
- Drop me a line and let me know what you are really passionate about.

Life as a business person, an entrepreneur or a Trustee does not have to be a lonely experience. You are not alone, and the support framework is there for you to engage, contribute and grow forward from. All you have to do is reach out and introduce yourself - it starts with Hello!

37. SSAS ALLIANCE

"There are known knowns. These are things
we know that we know.
There are known unknowns. These are things
that we know we don't know.
But there are also unknown unknowns.
These are things we don't know we don't know"

Donald Rumsfeld

As I became a SSAS Trustee for the first time, the weight of responsibility and accountability for not only my own pension pot but also for those of my fellow Trustees, was not lost on me.

My fellow Trustees and I were acutely aware that whilst we had undertaken exhaustive due diligence and were comfortable with our decision to establish a SSAS, we still felt that we had some blind sides, didn't fully understand what was in the art of the possible and quite frankly had that feeling of not knowing what we didn't know!

We decided that we would become blackbelts in SSAS management. We owed that to ourselves, to each other and our future generations as SSAS Trustees. We have always been involved in creating and operating highly collaborative organisations and cultures and it quickly became clear that others were equally finding fundamental questions they wanted to ask in order to increase their knowledge and experience with others.

The SSAS Alliance was born.

We set out to create a truly independent leading light organisation that is dedicated to supporting Trustees and those interested in exploring SSAS pensions to establish knowledge, collaboration, connection and contribution in their SSAS journey.

As Trustees we are:

- Only competing with what we are capable of
- Absorbing knowledge and identifying how to master its application
- Sharing ideas and knowledge
- Inspiring and motivating others
- Gain confidence and momentum
- Creating forming great relationships

Many Trustees I meet are also entrepreneurs and I think many would agree that entrepreneurship can feel a lonely business at times. Maybe it is the level of accountability, the responsibility of making all decisions and the thrill of success - or the evolution of building on lessons learnt from less successful decisions.

Wherever that feeling comes from, what was very clear was that this sense of camaraderie was highly valued by our initial members and since those formative stages SSAS Alliance has grown exponentially and now establish as the largest collaborative SSAS community in the country.

Our members are regularly connecting, learning, sharing and engaging in amazing opportunities and we have seen members raise significant funds for their ventures. One development company raised £2,000,000 of SSAS Trustee investment in one day as a fantastic example of creating shared value.

The SSAS Alliance arranges events and meetings across the country to enable SSAS to become more understood and to ensure that those interested understand the accountability that comes with SSAS and approach it in a responsible manner, equipped with the connections, knowledge and approach to support them in their growth.

It is the passion, drive and collaboration that defines many of our members and the resonance of personal qualities, ethics and a shared long-term vision that really has created formations of friendships that will remain for a life time and possibly become multi-generational.

Now that is something truly special to behold.

Our members are now connecting on a regular basis at our regional SSAS Alliance Business Networking events where local meetings are held on a monthly basis.

You can find your local meeting event at www.SSASalliance.org

Why not join our rapidly expanding membership and enjoy the connection and collaboration as you explore your passion for seizing ownership of your personal economy **CREATING EXTRAORDINARY LEVELS OF COMPOUNDING WEALTH?**

38. TRUSTEE CONTINUOUS PROFESSIONAL DEVELOPMENT

"The function of education is to teach one to think intensively and to think critically.
Intelligence plus character - that is the goal of true education"

Martin Luther King, Jr.

As you will have seen throughout this book, the obligations and responsibilities of being a Trustee of your SSAS are highly accountable, clear and should be taken seriously. The balance to the equation though is the pleasure, control, freedom and choice that you have in finally managing the last remaining part of your personal economy for many decades to come.

Given the incredible opportunity that awaits you and the responsibility in defining your own destiny, it would make sense to fully equip yourself, early in the process, to learning and educating yourself in order to master every angle surrounding the possibilities and approaches with a SSAS.

Continuous Professional Development (CPD) is the term used to describe the learning activities that professionals engage in to develop and enhance their abilities. It enables learning to become conscious and proactive, rather than passive and reactive.

CPD combines different methodologies to learning from theory based to practical, such as training workshops, conferences and events, e-learning programs, best practice techniques and ideas sharing, all focused for an individual to improve and have effective professional development.

There are fresh opportunities to seek out, new relationships to forge and yes, risks to manage along the way. The following three areas will enable you to grow yourself in this remarkable sphere of wealth stimulation and creation:

1. Surrounding yourself with a great community of like-minded knowledgeable people, possibly at one of our SSAS Alliance Business Network regional events.

2. Engaging with professional resources who will assist you in the compliance and governance of your SSAS.

3. Continuous Professional Development – Learning, education, minimising the 'I don't know what I don't know' areas. Growing yourself – becoming articulate, knowledgeable and confident in what you are doing.

SSAS Alliance can support you in accessing the information, support, education and confidence that you will need to drive optimum performance, maximum control and compliance and minimum time input.

The subject of SSAS is compelling for many and can be complex - but as the quote from Chinese philosopher Lao Tzu illustrates:

"A journey of a thousand miles begins with a single step"

What will your first steps look like?

39. FINAL THOUGHTS

"Dare to live the life you have dreamed for yourself. Go forward and make your dreams come true"

Ralph Waldo Emerson

I wrote this book to become your constant companion and north star as you follow your SSAS strategy.

It is unique and first of a kind, revealing the detail of this hitherto, little known HMRC and government backed strategy.

My wish is that it has started to ignite the passion in you. The passion for you to immerse yourself in the detail, to become fully equipped and prepared to seize control of your personal economy and to establish the benefits of your SSAS for many years, perhaps decades to come.

In my first 25 working years of my career, pensions did not excite me one bit!

I found them dull and they held little interest. However, I hope this book has illustrated to you the clear and present connection you could, and should make, between your pension and your personal economy and how you can actively engage in connecting them NOW.

My vision for this book is to connect people with possibility. To ensure that SSAS will be better understood, as will the responsibilities of being a Trustee, and that the necessary business management skills, education and compliance will be embraced with gusto.

Living life on your own terms can and is achievable. Looking back on your life you have probably achieved so much already, however why stop there. In the words of Jesse Itzler,

"You Didn't Come This Far…To Only Come This Far"

Why wait until you retire to sample the joys of choice, freedom and all the pleasures that can bring? Whether you have a pension or not, SSAS and the wisdom and experience contained in this book will be a valuable roadmap for you to assess your current circumstances, contemplate and define your strategy and then execute with clarity and passion.

In my humble opinion a truly optimised and enriched life of purpose is powerful beyond pleasure in optimising your physical and mental well-being. It can create a deep sense of satisfaction that you have established very significant steps along the path towards vast growth of compounding wealth for decades, maybe even centuries to come.

I hope you will have found the stark realisation emerging in these pages that creating the wealth and the compounding towards an exponential growth is only one part of SSAS, in the same way that money is only one part of the wealth of life.

Ensuring that this growth becomes a force for good is another thing entirely. Wealth only magnifies the person you are and the values you stand true to.

How will you amplify your values as a congruent part of your legacy?

Our personal growth, education, mind-set, continuous transformation and evolution is essential to keep up with the ever-changing world along with the risk and opportunity that will inevitably come in this increasingly ultra-high speed, connected economy we live in.

As we have seen throughout the book, you must establish solid foundations for you to anchor the basics to and build upwards and outwards from there.

"You can't fire a cannon from a canoe" – the same is the case for any business plan including your SSAS.

As the old saying goes – "Be general in your foundations and be specific in your goals"

How will you take those formative steps to embracing your pension strategy?

Yes, SSAS comes with a strong level of accountability, but no more so than in any other business opportunity and it can be understood and mastered by many, as long as you have knowledge, application, mind-set and strategy all aligned.

The staggering array of opportunity that a SSAS and its radiating possibilities present in economic wealth terms is matched by the opportunity for each of us to grow in stature, confidence, humility and passion.

It also represents a golden opportunity to start the process of equipping our children and their children with the skills, confidence and gravitas to be responsible and accountable in becoming the custodians of our legacy.

There can be no finer feeling than to see our future generations grow in stature and experience to become a better version of ourselves, a unique version of themselves and handsomely equipped to forge and harness the awaiting opportunities that beckon in the decades ahead.

When you connect people and opportunity, money can flow at an alarming rate and at incredible volumes - and flow it must! Money only serves a purpose and creates growth if it flows and the faster the velocity the more opportunity it can create.

Take as an example the £2m that we raised within 24 hours on our South East development through SSAS funds. When great people see great opportunity to create shared value, the possibilities become endless and hugely compelling.

I hope this book has equipped you with the ability to ask better questions, to enable you to get better answers and results. This will form a crucial part of your bank grade due diligence, essential in managing risk and preserving and growing your capital investments.

I see SSAS as a strategy for people who answer to their own standards.

With the information and guidance within these pages and with the support of the SSAS Alliance, you will be many steps closer to unlocking the vast array of incredible benefits to **CREATING EXTRAORDINARY LEVELS OF COMPOUNDING WEALTH.**

I strongly suggest that you re-read this book, make notes, highlight lines, fold page corners and write over it etc. This book is destined to be the dog-eared book that sits, not neatly on your book shelf, but on your table always within constant reach of you, as a source of knowledge, guidance and inspiration.

Once you have done this and built your action plan then you can start to define your own story and start writing the next exciting chapters of your personal wealth economy.

Newton's first law of motion states that "an object at rest stays at rest, and an object in motion stays in motion with the same speed and in the same direction unless acted upon by an unbalanced force."

The crucial action for you is to make a start. Without action nothing can change and progress.

Do not feel you have to become a black belt on day one – this is a life changing course of action and the learning will accumulate and compound over many years from this point, but only if you choose to make a start now.

The timing will never be perfect, sometimes you have to commit to the goal, make a start and figure things out along the way.

I would not agree to this in every circumstance, given my risk management background, but I absolutely get the logic.

You would not wait until all the traffic lights were on green before you left the house on a journey.

There is never an ideal time for anything in life. It is for us to identify the opportunity, seize the moment, become relentless in our pursuit, carve out the time, passion and focus to want to transform ourselves – that for me is freedom of choice.

I would genuinely like to hear from you about your progress and your thoughts on the book, so please drop me a line at mark.stokes@equaSSAS.co.uk or come along to one of our SSAS Alliance Business Network events.

I wish you all the very best in your exciting future.

40. ANOTHER BOOK BY THE AUTHOR

COMMERCIAL TO RESIDENTIAL CONVERSIONS
The essential manual for property developers

Whether you are new to business, property and investing, or taking your business to the next level, this indispensable development manual will guide you through the systems and processes required for Commercial to Residential Conversions.

It is written BY a developer, FOR developers and invaluable FOR investor 'Bank Grade Due Diligence'.

Mark shares in-depth insights on what it really takes to succeed, what makes him tick, his personal journey and very personal reflections on creating a sustainable, high performance business enabling YOU to achieve those highly profitable results.

Are you serious about:

- Building a high-performance culture in your business?
- Achieving outstanding results whilst managing risk?
- Understanding the detailed steps and systems?
- Ensuring Bank Grade Due Diligence?
- Maximising compliance and security?
- Making a start with confidence?
- Creating massive shared value?

This manual is required reading and will be your vital companion as you master this strategy and grow your profitable business.

If you are interested in attending Mark's two-day Advanced Commercial Developers' Masterclass, more details can be found at www.markstokesuk.com/events

41. ABOUT THE AUTHOR

As an experienced Business Executive, Entrepreneur and Investor, Mark has a passion for creating and developing enduring businesses that enable the creation of shared value. With 26 years of board level business and property expertise in data centres, energy, construction and telecommunication industries, Mark has founded and operated many businesses, home and abroad, deploying complex global infrastructure projects from £1million - £1billion. Mark is a highly sought-after business mentor and speaker with vast experience internationally in risk management, leadership, trouble shooting and business - from founding, acquiring and growing through to selling a business.

Having sold his equity in a leading management business and then leaving corporate life in 2015, Mark established a number of pioneering investment and development companies.

Having career long company pensions, Mark set out to explore different opportunities to take control of his personal economy and quickly settled on a SSAS which is now an active part of his long-term investment and wealth creation strategy.

Mark and Sharon are proud parents of four wonderful children: Ben, Jack, Katy and Emily.

Mark has a passion and ethos for creating shared and sustainable value through property, investments and building a powerful and enduring legacy for future generations.

Mark has mentored people for 20 years and has been a Non-Executive Director for over a decade. Mark specialises in Business, Commercial Property Investment and Development and SSAS pensions.

If you are interested in knowing more about mentorship, email Mark directly at mark.stokes@equaSSAS.co.uk.

To connect with Mark, check out his personal website

www.markstokesuk.com

Mark and business partner Nigel Greene, established SSAS Alliance to promote and support fellow SSAS Trustees through collaboration, connection and learning.

Find out more at www.SSASalliance.org

SSAS

ALLIANCE

42. SSAS BUSINESS PODCAST

If you are inspired by the book and looking to keep up to date then Mark's SSAS BUSINESS PODCAST is essential listening.

The podcast airs weekly and features lively interviews, features and content ensuring you are kept up to date, inspired and refreshed on all things SSAS and Business. We cover current and relevant subjects in detail including:

SSAS pensions and what you need to know

- Business interviews and discussion
- Interviews featuring case studies of SSAS in action
- Ideas, thoughts and wisdom on investment decision making
- Inspiration on lifestyle for business entrepreneurs and SSAS Trustees

GLOSSARY

AA	-	Annual Allowance
ASA	-	Administration Service Agreement
AVC	-	Additional Voluntary Contribution
BCE	-	Benefit Crystallisation Event
CETV	-	Cash Equivalent Transfer Value
CPD	-	Continuous Professional Development
CSV	-	Creating Shared Value
DB	-	Defined Benefit
DC	-	Defined Contribution
DCC	-	Double Compound Curve
FCA	-	Financial Conduct Authority
FRI	-	Full Repair and Insure Lease
FSCS	-	Financial Services Compensation Scheme
GDCV	-	Genuinely Diverse Commercial Vehicle
GUF	-	General Unallocated Fund
HMRC	-	Her Majesty's Revenue and Customs
ICO	-	Information Commissioners Office
ICVC	-	Investment Company with Variable Capital
IHT	-	Inheritance Tax
LLP	-	Limited Liability Partnership
LTA	-	Lifetime Allowance
LTV	-	Loan to Value
MPAA	-	Money Purchase Annual Allowance

OEIC	-	Open-Ended Investment Company
P2P	-	Peer to Peer
PPF	-	Pension Protection Fund
PTM	-	Pensions Tax Manual
REIT	-	Real Estate Investment Trust
RoTE	-	Return on Time Employed
RICS	-	Royal Institute of Chartered Surveyors
SDLT	-	Stamp Duty Land Tax
SIPP	-	Self Invested Personal Pension
SME	-	Small to Medium Enterprise
SoIP	-	Statement of Investment Principles
SSAS	-	Small Self-Administered Scheme
TPAS	-	The Pensions Advisory Service
TPR	-	The Pension Regulator
VAT	-	Value Added Tax

HELPFUL LINKS

SSAS Alliance	www.SSASalliance.org
Our development company	www.equagroup.co.uk
My personal website	www.markstokesuk.com
The Pension Regulator	www.thepensionsregulator.gov.uk
Pension Tax Manual	https://www.gov.uk/hmrc-internal-manuals/pensions-tax-manual/ptm121000
Investments in Shares and Equities	https://www.gov.uk/hmrc-internal-manuals/pensions-tax-manual/ptm122000
Loans and general principles	https://www.gov.uk/hmrc-internal-manuals/pensions-tax-manual/ptm123100
Pension Ombudsman Service - Pensions Ombudsman Helpline 020 7630 2200	https://www.pensionwise.gov.uk/en/guaranteed-income
The Pension Ombudsman	www.pensions-ombudsman.org.uk
The Financial Conduct Authority	https://register.fca.org.uk
The Money Advice Service	https://www.moneyadviceservice.org.uk/en

The Governments Actuary's Department	https://www.gov.uk/ government/organisations/ government-actuarys-department
The Pension Tax Manual	https://www.gov.uk/hmrc-internal-manuals/pensions-tax-manual

Your notes:

Your Notes:

Your Notes: